Experiencing the Hero's Journey

Experiencing The Hero's Journey
Foolish Wisdom Book 1: An Apprentice of Wonder

by
Joseph Riggio, Ph.D.

Parrhesia Ink Publishing
Princeton ▪ New Jersey

Copyright © 2014 Joseph Riggio
All rights reserved.

First Printing

Published by:
Parrhesia Ink Publishing
Princeton, New Jersey

Cover Design by: Red Sanderson

Printed in the United State of America

No part of this book may be reproduced, translated, stored in a retrieval system, or transmitted in any form or by any means, including but not limited to electronic, mechanical, photocopying, microfilming, recording or otherwise without prior expressed written permission from the publisher.

Library of Congress Cataloging-in-Publication Data

Joseph Riggio, Ph.D.
    Experiencing The Hero's Journey
    Foolish Wisdom Book 1: An Apprentice of Wonder

Includes bibliographical references and other resources

LCCN: 2014910037
ISBN: 0-69222-983-3

Self-Help / Personal Growth / General

Dedication:

to

Nancy S. Riggio

with love

CONTENTS

Acknowledgements   v.
Foreword: W.L. Hoffman, J.D.   ix.
Author's Preface: Joseph Riggio, Ph.D.   xiii.

Introduction   1
    The Blue Dell Farm "Hypnotorium"   3
    Preppy to Iconoclastic Outcast   4
    Waking From The Dream   8

1 - Stepping Off The Path   13
    "I Want To Believe …"   15
    Catching The Training Flu   18
    Going To The Dogs   25

2 - Answering The Call   31
    Crossing The Threshold   33
    Confronting The Crisis   37
    "Toto, I've A Feeling We're Not In Kansas Anymore"   40

3 - A New Way Of Learning   45
    Interstellar Zen Tales   47
    Phrasing and P(2)hrasing   52
    Psychic Rapport, Psychopaths & Whole-Form Learning   55

4 - The Chalice And The Crucible — 63
Swallowing The Canary Whole — 65
Ontologically Speaking … — 71
Beginning To Become Myself Again — 78

5 - The Game Called, "Life" — 83
Illusions And Delusions — 85
"The Game Is Afoot" — 90
Seeing Beyond Illusion — 95

6 - Soul Relief — 99
Growing Up "Italian" — 101
Early Mis-Education — 106
Bringing The System To Rest — 112

7 - Harnessing Chaos — 119
NLP And Hypnosis At The Pond — 121
Hypnotic Protocol In Communication — 126
Nominalization, States, And Magic — 131

8 - The Abyss — 139
Ontological Distress — 141
Crashing, Burning … And Rebuilding — 144
Regaining A Sense Of Sanity — 149

9 - Going Beyond The Story — 155
Freezing (Your Ass Off) In Hell — 157
Separation From Self — 161
Distinctions Of Distress — 166

10 - Owning Your Adventure — 173
The Story Of Your Life — 175
The Terror And Thrill Of Discovery — 182
Losing My Mind … And Finding It Again — 187

Epilogue — 199
Living In Wonder — 201

Afterword — 205
Beyond The Paradox — 207

Further Resources — 215
Recommended Reading — 217
Beyond The Books … — 225
About The Author — 229
The State of Perfection — 233

ACKNOWLEDGEMENTS

Every author writes the same thing at the start of a book ... "This book would not have been possible without the efforts of ..." or "It is not possible to write a book by yourself ..." or maybe "Every author knows that no book is written alone ..." or some such thing. The reason they write something like this is because it is true. The actual writing of a book may be a solo effort, but getting the finished product you are now reading into the hands of readers is another thing entirely ... that takes a crowd!

The first part of the crowd I'd like to acknowledge and thank are all of the giants whose shoulders I stand on that came before me. A good list to begin with are all the authors I mention in the "Recommended Reading" section at the back of the book. However there are couple I want to point out in particular. The first is a man whom I never met, Joseph Campbell, but who nonetheless was a mentor of mine from afar. In his writing and recorded lectures I feel like I came to know Joseph Campbell and learned much from what he had to say. Another is Dr. Richard Bandler whom I have had the pleasure and honor of meeting and learning from in person. His work is seminal, and the work I have developed is built upon much of the groundwork he and his collaborator, Dr. John Grinder, put in place known collectively as neurolinguistic programming, or NLP. A personal friend of my mine, John La Valle, introduced me to Richard Bandler's work in my early days of learning the material and I remain indebted to him for his teaching and his friendship as well.

The final and most significant of my teachers that I want to acknowledge here is Roye Fraser, who you will meet many times throughout this book. It was through his prodding, provocation, teaching, guiding, mentoring and friendship that I am able to write the book you hold in your hands today. His work was brilliant and when the opportunity presented itself I immediately accepted his unspoken invitation to pursue the journey to becoming an apprentice of wonder. Roye's work was instrumental in my coming to know myself as I do, and in learning how to offer others the opportunity to explore the Adventure, becoming apprentices of wonder in their own right.

It pleases me to share a few more names with you that were somehow involved in my journey to getting to where I am today, and the writing of this book. There were the friends and confidants that contributed to my early conviction that I had something of value to share, like David Newlin, whom I inadvertently did not mention in my first book **State of Perfection: Your Hidden Code to Unleashing Personal Mastery** and one of the first folks to help me build a platform to strut my stuff. There are a few I also want to mention because of the impact they have had on this particular work. Bob Brandau my friend who taught me how to walk a dog. Bill Hoffman, attorney, author and personal foil. Charles Moore for always showing delight when I offer him my work to read and edit. Michael Cage who alternatively badgers me into taking action and believes in the action I take, like writing this book. My dear friend and personal confidant Laura McFarland for showing interest as I kept emailing pieces of the manuscript as they were completed and encouraging me to keep going ⋯ even when I was merely complaining about being on my final, final, final, final, final edit ⋯ and the one after that too. And, last but surely not least, my brilliant graphic designer Red Sanderson who created the cover concept and produced the artwork for it. There are others I have met along the way to getting to where I am in my life today, too many to mention here and not make the acknowledgement pages a book unto itself.

I would be remiss if I did not also take a moment to mention my family who are always there, in the foreground and in the background in all I do … especially my beloved children Jason and Michaela, parents, Francesco and Assunta (Chick and Sue), my brother Louis and his wife Ingrid, my nieces Gabriella and Francesca, my father-in-law Lee and his wife Beverly, my brother-in-law Hank and his wife Joy, and my niece Lilly Rose (the little flower in the family), my nieces Leela and Gracie, and their parents Ruth and Bill too … all part of the clan I call my family, along with too many aunts, uncles and cousins to mention here … all part and parcel of the cacophony of love and laughter I get to partake of each time we gather … thank you all from the bottom of my heart for being who you are always.

ACKNOWLEDGEMENTS

To all of those I have not mentioned, my apologies ... but I assure you, you are neither forgotten nor overlooked ... and you know who you are without me having to write all about it ... including you.

With profound affection and appreciation,

Joseph Riggio
Princeton, N.J. 2013

PRODUCTION NOTES:
(For all my technical and behind the scenes readers)

I wrote this book on an **Apple 13" MacBook Pro** using **Scrivener** writing software from **Literature and Latte** - the best writing tool out there for authors as far as I am concerned, and I use many. The font I chose to work in was **Calibri Regular** 12 pt. because it was easy on my eyes as I wrote and I like it as a digital font as well. I used **Minon Pro** in various point sizes ranging from 9 pt. To 18 pt. for printing because, again, it is easy on the eye as printed text and I think it is a beautiful font to work with as well.

Foolish Wisdom Book 1: Experiencing the Hero's Journey was written almost entirely at at table in the back southeast corner of **It's a Grind** coffeehouse in Plainsboro, NJ. over many mugs of good black coffee. "My table" was just in front of and beneath a painting of Billie Holiday and facing two others of Bruce "The Boss" Springsteen and Eric "Slow Hand" Clapton. They were unendingly gracious about my taking up that space day after day for the cost of a couple cups of coffee - and they even threw in free Internet so I could do research and upload my writing too!

FOREWORD: W.L. HOFFMAN, J.D.

Suppose everything you thought you knew about "who" you are and "what" you know is an illusion. Worse, what if it's an imprint that's been fed to you masquerading as an innocuous template before you had any ability to identify it and defend yourself? Perhaps, you now simply feel like you're stuck in a rut or perpetually in "search" mode. Alternatively, you might be a productive and successful member of society, financially stable, in a solid relationship and bearing all the hallmarks of the "good" life. And yet, there's a tickling in the back of your mind, an itch that strikes in the quiet hours, when the white noise of life abates and you only hear the whispers from within. I walked upon that road. I'm an Ivy League trained attorney that "jumped" the tracks.

If you prefer a more contextual metaphor, I awoke from The Matrix – as depicted in the science fiction movie written by the Wachowskis. There was no mentor offering me the choice of swallowing the red or blue pill, and thus overtly choosing my reality. For thirty years, I moved in sync with other's expectations. I excelled in school, graduated with honors, obtained my Juris Doctorate, married the love of my life, and had a successful law practice at a prominent firm in Princeton, NJ… but there was the itch. I knew that I needed to step off that career path, but not necessarily "why." I gave the firm my two week's notice. My goal then was to observe the world on "my" time, and to position myself with the freedom of "mind and body" to embrace other possibilities. This ultimately led me to a more "present" life and to pursuing a passion that ran through my blood from my earliest memories. You see, I am fascinated by the fantastic, and my dreams have always transported me to strange realms. Each literary wonderland that I opened – whether it was one of classic adventure, mystery, mythology, fantasy, sci-fi, supernatural or romance - was my personal portal to a new existence. If you haven't guessed it already, I began to write stories.

My preferred genres are that of science fiction and fantasy. While I studied English literature and philosophy in college, I never enrolled in a course covering the Hero's Journey as conceptualized by the famous mythologist Joseph Campbell. Instead, I was intuitively immersed within that model over a lifetime of reading, watching movies, attending theatre and living my own adventures. The irony of the situation was that I was so cognitively blind for so long to this pattern that was staring me in the face.

And so it was, about eight years ago, that I came to meet Dr. Joseph Riggio. Our wives had already formed a bond through our choice of alternative education for our respective daughters – The Waldorf School. Eventually, at my wife's urging, I bumped into Joseph at a Parents' Night gathering. The exchange was brief, and there was no secret handshake, but in those minutes, we "recognized" each other. Shortly thereafter, I asked Joseph what he did to earn a living. It was a simple enough conversation starter, or so I thought. Initially, I understood him to be a consultant. That perception slowly drifted into a trendy moniker that I applied incorrectly to him: "life coach." Somewhat later, after realizing that my nomenclature for Joseph was inaccurate, I described him to friends as a motivational speaker facilitating exceptional performance for businesses and individuals. Over the years, we had family outings, exchanged anecdotes, plunged into the Universe, shared insights on the human condition and deconstructed public policy.

Throughout my time with Joseph, my conception of his work was continually evolving. That's an amazing pronouncement. How many people do you know that after years of friendship, you still can't pinpoint what they do in the world? So there I stood, with not quite a decade between us. With the experience of things spoken and unspoken, had someone asked me about the "magic" Joseph did with folks, I could have confidently stated that I at least had a rudimentary understanding of his transformational technique: the MythoSelf Process. After all that time, as incredible as it seems, I never quite managed the "Aha!" moment... Joseph's "story" remained elusive to my grasp.

In this Foolish Wisdom book, Joseph finally "pulls back the curtain" in a powerful format that no single training session could possibly convey. The writing is intentionally sculpted with methodology – Whole Form Learning, Whole Form Communication, achieving a Ready

FORWARD

State – and while some of the material easily absorbs, some will require looping contemplation. He begins with a question each of us should ask: **"Who am I?"** The answer is contained within his journey, and you are invited to ride along, as a master unveils his teachings. For some, this might be like discovering a hidden trail marker upon a suspected path, but for others, I have no doubt that Joseph's story will engender a pivotal life moment that resets and forever changes your "awareness" and choice of reality.

W.L. Hoffman, J.D.

Author of:
The Soulstealer War: The First Mother's Fire

AUTHOR'S PREFACE: JOSEPH RIGGIO, PH.D.

Jessep: *You want answers?*
Kaffee: *I think I'm entitled to them.*
Jessep: *You want answers?*
Kaffee: ***I want the truth!***
Jessep: ***You can't handle the truth!***
Jessep (continues): *Son, we live in a world that has walls. And those walls have to be guarded by men with guns. Who's gonna do it? You? You, Lt. Weinberg? I have a greater responsibility than you can possibly fathom. You weep for Santiago and you curse the Marines. You have that luxury. You have the luxury of not knowing what I know: that Santiago's death, while tragic, probably saved lives. And my existence, while grotesque and incomprehensible to you, saves lives ... You don't want the truth. Because deep down, in places you don't talk about at parties, you want me on that wall. You need me on that wall. We use words like honor, code, loyalty...we use these words as the backbone to a life spent defending something. You use 'em as a punch line. I have neither the time nor the inclination to explain myself to a man who rises and sleeps under the blanket of the very freedom I provide, then questions the manner in which I provide it! I'd rather you just said thank you and went on your way. Otherwise, I suggest you pick up a weapon and stand a post.* ***Either way, I don't give a damn what you think you're entitled to!***

From: **"A Few Good Men"** by Aaron Sorkin

This is a storybook. All I really ever speak or write about are stories. Do not waste your time looking for truth. But, like any good story, it has the potential to transform. As the renowned mythologist Joseph Campbell taught us, ultimately every story told is a story about

Adventure. When the story is well told it depersonalizes the individual dream, transforming it to myth ... and transforming us in turn.

The kind of story I tell here has transformational power because it is not written in a way that makes ordinary sense. It is not even written for your ordinary mind.

This story is written for your "Silent Mind."

Your "Silent Mind" is poetic, not prosaic. Consider what you are about to read like you would an ancient epic poem, like Homer's "The Iliad" or "The Odyssey" ... or Dante's "Divine Comedy." There are more modern versions of the epic like Joyce's revolutionary "Ulysseus" or his impenetrable "Finnegan's Wake." Maybe you would prefer something more specifically cultural, like Germany's "Doctor Faust" by Thomas Mann ... Russia's "The Brother's Karamozov" by Dostoevesky ... or America's "The Great Gatsby" by Fitzgerald. Each of these stories flows within the structure of mythic form ... making sense at the surface level by speaking to our conscious mind, and also stirring something more primitive and primal in our sub-conscious mind. These stories are designed to reawaken something in us, and the best of them reawaken us to ourselves.

While I cannot claim to stand in the ranks of the great author's like those I mention above, I am aiming to copy what they have done through the ages for readers ... to write a story that satisfies your conscious mind, while stirring something deeper, to help you awaken to yourself again. This is the magic of myth, and the mythic form on which it is based. Myth reawakens you to yourself in new ways that are familiar to you because they are really old ways for you. Though it may seem nonsensical, the new ways I refer to are in reality ways that were familiar to you before they were eradicated by what I call "bad learning."

Bad learning is everything that forces us to ignore our deepest intuitions. We are born with the ability to learn how to survive, prosper and thrive. This ability is literally our birthright as human beings, but it comes with a caveat ... we must choose to become fully human. Our species made a deal with nature. Unlike insects or reptiles emerging from their eggs ready to live out their life "as is," humans sacrifice coming out of the womb fully formed and complete, for the ability to learn from birth to death. We are capable of becoming what we will in our lives by virtue of our ability to learn, each generation seemingly able to move beyond the limits of the past, by learning from it.

As we create progress, building on the learning of the past, we also create complexity. The solution we came up with to the problem of greater complexity has been to tap into our natural capacity to learn. We built schools and formalized the learning process. Today children are forced to learn what they need to know to become productive members of society. Because of the complex systems we now live in, rather than just letting our children explore their world and find their way, we constrain children to learning along the lines that serves society best ... not necessarily themselves. After many years of this kind of conditioning, and the natural instincts it extinguishes, most people respond to life in a lock-step, knee jerk fashion ... stuck in place by the learning they were led to believe would free them.

I wrote this book to open up the pathways that will allow you to regain access to your earliest instincts and intuitions. When you know how the learning you have received ... and have probably come to think represents reality as you know it ... is coded, you can choose what to keep and what to update. Maybe for the first time, since you were an infant, you will be free to choose how to think for yourself. This is part of the gift of becoming fully human ... the freedom to choose for yourself.

The freedom to choose for yourself is a magnificent gift life bestows upon you at birth. The gift of learning to choose is often wrenched away before you can grasp it for yourself. Seeing your way clear to having the experience of your life, as you want it to be and not as others have designed and imposed it upon you, is like literally receiving a new lease on life. My writing is based on the years I spent in my own journey, the learning I received from many masters, including one remarkable teacher in particular, my many years working with thousands of clients ... and, much of what I now find myself doing and writing about is also supported by the latest findings in neuroscience.

If you read this book with a mind open to change you may find that it speaks to you in ways you would not have imagined could be possible from a mere book. It may seem unbelievable to think that reading a storybook could do all that I am suggesting, but it has been this way since our first ancestors emerged from the primordial forests and savannahs. Every culture, from time immemorial, has used stories to shape and change minds. The most powerful of these stores use mythic form. I have organized the stories you will read about in this book using mythic form too. While I was not the one to come up with the structure of myth, I am clever enough to use it to make my writing far more powerful than it could possibly be otherwise.

So here you are ... at the start of my story of transformation, beginning with my descent into insanity. Through the multiple twists and turns of my story, including virtually meeting many of the characters I came across, you may be reminded of your own journey ... one you had, the one you are on, or one you are about to undertake. In any case you are likely to find moments that resonate with you, when you do stop for a moment and ask yourself the question, **"Why does this particular thing seem to stand out from the background of the story for me?"** Do not worry about answering the question; any answer you come up with will be processed consciously. I am pointing you toward your Silent Brain, outside of your ordinary conscious awareness. I am hoping to open you again to instincts and intuitions repressed by years of "bad learning" ... to take back control of your own story ... to regain the poetry in your life.

Since this is just a storybook anyway, allow yourself to read it like one, without any expectation of it "making sense" beyond the story it tells. You will not find a profound step-by-step process you can use to transform your life. You will not find clever examples or anecdotes that make my point clear. I have not used little life vignettes to convince you that what I am presenting works using social proof. There are not any glowing testimonials about how wonderful my work or I am. You will just have to read it, get what you get, and trust yourself ... it is a lot to ask, I know, but when you have you will no longer need the experts who would tell you otherwise.

It would be more than presumptuous to assume that anyone could be a greater expert on you than yourself, and I am not that presumptuous. Instead of trying to reveal you to you, I will stick with an area where I am an expert, revealing me to you. In sharing a part of my story with you maybe you will discover a hidden bit of your own story. By the time you have finished reading my story you will also know something about the process that led me from my presumed sanity into a descent to a kind of social insanity. From my time spent being "insane" we will travel back again together to what I now think of as a remarkably sane state ... maybe even more sane than society tells us is possible.

AUTHOR'S PREFACE

Along the way, as we journey together in this book, in revealing the process I experienced ... the twists, turns and the details ... you will learn something about what story is and how it works. While there were more moments than I wish to remember where the process seemed to be utterly chaotic at the time, I realize now, looking back on them, that most of those moments were perfectly choreographed. By stepping beyond my story I will include some of what I have learned as a result of living it. Between reading about me in my tale ... and about some of the learning I accumulated along the way ... you will have everything you need to revisit, refine and rewrite your own story. A huge boon that you will get as well, will be that you will be able to use the learning you gain about storytelling for yourself ... and with others too ... if you choose it.

Just like every good story ever told, my loosely formed memoir, contains the truth, the whole truth and nothing but the truth ... or at least it points to it even when as the author I did not know that myself. Of course, the trick to making the story work for you is finding the truth within yourself ... especially if the truth is a story you have been avoiding for too long.

One final thing and I'll set you free to experience the Adventure for yourself. I cannot strongly enough recommend that simply let yourself be taken by my story as you would by any piece of fictional prose, or maybe by words and acts of a great lover ...

Joseph Riggio, Ph.D.
Princeton, New Jersey 2013

Introduction:
The Journey Begins

"Be Good ... Fit In"
- Joseph Riggio

INTRODUCTION

The Blue Dell Farm "Hypnotorium"

My head lolled forward and it was possible that I was drooling a bit ... completely at peace and feeling great, sitting with my eyes closed on a stool in front of a room full of strangers. I was in the "Hypnotorium" at the Blue Dell Farm in Pemberton, N.J. situated on the edge of the New Jersey Pine Barrens. Next to me was a man, a little larger than life, whom I just met a few minutes earlier ... Roye, a South-African Jew who had spent the last twenty-five years or so as an Israeli commando. It was quite a scene I had gotten myself into ... more than I could have possibly guessed was true at the time.

The group in the Hypnotorium was about as varied as I could imagine any group being and still remaining in the same room together. I remember the woman who prompted me to show up, a dark haired pleasant lady, "Linda," who was a true believer as far as I could tell. There was also the Upper East Side New York City investment banker who seemed alternately agitated and remarkably peaceful in turns. Also, from New York City, but from down in the East Village, was the gay man struggling with relationship issues.

There were folks from New York, New Jersey, Connecticut, Massachusetts, California, Texas, Canada, London, Israel and South Africa ... about twenty in all as I remember it now. The group was a global gang of characters, each and every one. Another woman I met there was a yoga instructor. A little later on, I met a couple of others as well ... an Orthodox Jewish diamond merchant, and a young Israel solider visiting the U.S. who had come specifically to do private work with Roye. There was a beautiful, young blond woman in the room too, though I never quite got where she was from or why she was there. It was a varied and sundry group, all seemingly intent on staring at me with my mouth hanging open, drooling in the front of the room as Roye went on and on.

I could not tell you what he was talking about today if my life depended on it. I recall rousing myself every once in a while and lifting my head up, beginning to open my eyes to look about. Each time I lifted my head, Roye would reach over, slide his hand down from my forehead to my chin, barely an inch or two in front of my face. As he did this he would gently speak, telling me things like, "Just close your eyes, relax ... sleep if you like ... there is nothing you need to do out here with us ... everything you want is all on the inside ... for you to find." This was my introduction to working with Roye Fraser, Master NLP Trainer and Hypnotist, in his "Hypnotorium" ... the space he had built for "doing work" with people and running programs like the one I was now in the midst of myself.

From Preppy to Iconoclastic Outcast

While I could not tell you what Roye said to me on my first day with him, I can tell you why I was in his Hypnotorium at the Blue Dell Farm in Pemberton, N.J. I had come to learn more about NLP*, a powerful personal change technology, developed by two geniuses who met at the University of California - Santa Cruz. The year before I had participated in an NLP Practitioner Certification training with two other trainers.

In the world of NLP, practitioner training is the basic starting point. I was now on a mission to complete my Master Practitioner Certification, on my way to earning full NLP Trainer Certification ... what I assumed would be a two year journey, give or take a couple of months ...

The reason I was on the journey however was because I was lost.

I would now argue, after more than two decades of guiding people in their own journeys, that realizing you're lost is often the perfect place to begin.

Keeping what could be a long history short, I was the product of a good middle class upbringing from a blue-collar neighborhood in N.J. A bit unusual for the neighborhood I grew up in, I had the privilege of a high-quality Catholic college preparatory secondary school education designed to prepare me to get into the university of my choice. Many of my peers from high-school went on to Ivy League universities, and a few went on to the elite U.S. Military Academies ... West Point, Annapolis, the

INTRODUCTION

U.S. Air Force Academy ... a rather extraordinary and impressive group of young men.

Seton Hall Preparatory High School was an all boys school ... in those days it was on the campus of Seton Hall University in South Orange, N.J. To make up for any lack of girls present in the school itself there were plenty of co-eds available on campus ... if you knew how to make that situation work for you.

The fact that I noticed there were "older" woman around, some of them who were interested in "younger" men, probably had something to do with my lack of interest in pursuing my education to the fullest at that time. I started out as a great student, finishing my first year near the very top of my high-school class. From that point on it was pretty much all downhill as I continued to lose interest in schooling with each passing year.

Despite my grand lack of interest I still managed to finish in the top quarter of my class, and was a National Merit Scholar semi-finalist, but I was totally uninterested in school. Nonetheless, I did what everyone expected of me and applied to college. I got accepted where I applied, and began relatively enthusiastically despite my general disinterest in getting any more formal education under my belt.

I was the typical American kid, a "baby boomer" from a stable working class family in the middle of the twentieth century, who had the opportunities to "get ahead in life" presented to me. At that time I believed, "getting a good education" was the path to creating a good life for myself, but my attention kept getting diverted, mostly by my own personal fascinations ... and of course, the girls. By the time I was in my last years of high school I was way more interested in the girls than in my education. Lucky me ... the girls were interested in me too. That was part of the problem.

In my last year at "The Prep," my senior year, I was cruising and prancing through life at one level ... popular, doing well enough to get by in all my classes, an active athlete who was also involved in multiple extracurricular activities. One of the most notable of my extracurricular activities in my senior year was starring in a spoof movie made by the drama department satirizing the incredibly successful "Rocky" film with Sylvester Stallone that had come out that year. They choose me because I bore a striking resemblance to the actor, and I was boxing competitively at the time. It also helped that I had a body like a young Adonis (it is hard to be humble when it is true ... but, that was a very long time ago now, so I can say it with a straight face and gracious humility).

What I did not know was that all the schooling in the world could not and would not save me from myself. There is no way to avoid walking your own path. There are really only two fundamental choices, 1) finding yourself and your way, or 2) living a life that is not your own. Partly by choice, and partly because I was thrust into it, I stepped off the pristine path presented to me and onto to another that led directly into the wilderness of uncertainty.

University never really worked well for me. While my friends were completing degrees, beginning their careers, or planning on attending graduate school, I was mostly floundering. I began a degree program in architecture that I never completed, but I was a quick enough study to pick up what I needed to get hired as an architectural draftsman by the time I was just eighteen going on nineteen.

By then I had already dropped out of college for all intents and purposes, although I was still registered for classes. I decided that although college was not for me, real education was, so I attended the classes I liked. I did this regardless of the application of the course to any degree program. I read the books assigned, asked a lot of questions, engaged in class discussions and debates, and did little else, i.e.: I neither took the tests, nor did the homework required to pass any of the classes I was taking. As a result I have an impressive list of diverse and varied university classes I have attended and failed ... at an equally impressive list of diverse and varied institutions. However, no one could stop me from benefiting from the education I was orchestrating for myself, despite their ability to grade me a failure and deny me a precious degree from their prestigious institute.

Believe me, there was a price to pay for the arrogance I displayed in my college years. A degree if nothing else is a ticket that opens doors that could otherwise remain locked to you. I found that out multiple times, and had to perform a bit of song and dance magic. It was also during this time that I learned to use trickster ways to get doors to open. One of those doors was getting hired as an architectural draftsman, then later on as an interior designer, and finally as an apprentice architect. All that occurred within the space of about four years. By the end of that span of time I was architecturally skilled. It seems what I lacked in my nature

INTRODUCTION

to submit to a formal education I more than made up for in my ability to absorb information and learn informally.

At the tender age of twenty-two, I was one of the founders of an interior architectural design firm with two partners. My specialty was doing interior architecture. Our practice, JS Randolph Associates, Inc. in Hackensack, N.J. did remarkably well. I was designing office spaces in some of the most prestigious buildings in New York City, including many, many commissions at Black Rock, the iconic CBS building on Sixth Avenue and 51st. I was also designing interiors for some of the most expensive apartments in New York City and homes along the bluffs overlooking the Hudson River in New Jersey, as well as others scattered throughout the area. These were productive, prosperous, good years. I was a full partner in a successful design firm, and I thought I was on top of the world, laughing all the way to the bank ... the joke however was on me.

In the next few years I broke up with a long-standing girlfriend that I wanted to marry, left the design firm I had founded with my partners, met another girl and was married within a year, stumbled around the design community for a couple of more years trying to find a place where I could settle down, had a beautiful baby boy, separated from my wife, moved back in with my parents, and started training dogs to pay the bills.

What a long, strange ride the few years from "successful young architect" to "failure at life" were ... a seismic event that shook the foundation of who I knew myself to be. The feeling of sliding down the slope from what seemed to be enormous success to what seemed to be cataclysmic failure, was like trying to stand during an earthquake, unable to find my footing. It was as though the earth beneath my feet was constantly shifting, offering me no place to stand securely for more than a few minutes at a time.

It was during this time that I found myself on that stool at the front of the room sitting next to Roye.

Note: *NLP = Neurolinguistic Programming

Waking From The Dream …

What I had thought was going to be a two year journey to obtaining an NLP Trainer Certification became a seven-year apprenticeship sitting at the knee of the master. From my point of view it was more like Army Ranger training, or Navy Seal boot camp, substituting the physical agony with mental and emotional agony. Of course there were a few intermittent "Hell Weeks" on occasion as well, for seven years running, but worth every minute looking back on it now. After the initial seven years of intense apprenticing with him, for an additional thirteen years I continued to benefit from Roye's experience and wisdom … as well as his friendship. From my side of the bargain Roye got to share his ideas with an able and willing student who had become a somewhat of a peer and colleague. Along the way, Roye got to vicariously experience some of the rewards of my journey presenting what I had been learning with him to audiences internationally.

Over those thirteen years, while Roye was still with us, I built a business taking the work into the highest level offices in business, government and non-profits internationally. I was invited to speak to groups as varied as an ASEAN economic development committee to the directors of summer camps at the American Camp Association's annual meeting. During this time I was writing articles for magazines, speaking on the radio and being interviewed on television. I presented at more NLP conferences and groups around the world than I can remember. I was also working privately, one-on-one, with individuals worldwide who wanted what I had to offer. The experience I was having led me to be constantly re-thinking everything I had learned and believed, including the model of work I was engaged in developing. Revisiting and refining the model continuously over the next ten years or so led to numerous interesting and deep conversations with Roye over many slices of pizza and countless cups of dark, hot coffee.

One of the outcomes of my learning with Roye, and working with clients worldwide, was the development of the model I originally called the Mythogenic Self Process and later shortened to the MythoSelf Process. The MythoSelf Process is a powerful, transformational changework model for individuals and organizations in transition. In part, I choose the name, "MythoSelf," as an homage to the renowned mythologist,

INTRODUCTION

Joseph Campbell. I did this because a significant part of my work was predicated on the Hero's Journey model that he had delineated years before. While my work was not directly mythological, i.e.: based on using the ancient myths that Joseph Campbell so masterfully told and used, it was - and is - definitely mythologically informed and organized. Rather than talking about mythology per se, I often refer to mythological or mythic form ... the essential way we know, understand and organize our subjective, phenomenological realities. The most obvious aspect of mythological or mythic form can be found in our autobiographic narrative ... what I call **"The Story of Your Life"** ... in which we contain our life experience metaphorically.

The MythoSelf Process model and work addresses how people organize the story of their lives as a "fictional autobiography," or more precisely a "fictional autobiographical narrative," that comes to represent reality, or truth, as they know it. Their fiction becomes the basis of their perceptions, sense-making, judgements, decision-making and behaviors. Anyone who believes their own autobiographical narrative however lives a fool's dream.

Nothing wrong with believing your own fictions per se, except when you can no longer tell the dream from being awake.

My "job" has largely become helping folks wake up and develop the strategies and skills they need to function, prosper and thrive in the world, while remaining fully awake ... in essence to become a "Wise Fool" living beyond the boundaries of the dream that constrains most folks to living "lives of quiet desperation."

People ask me why I use the phrase "Wise Fool" to refer to folks who have escaped the trap of the trivial that contains most folks in their day to day lives to "lives of quiet desperation" and there are many reasons I could give, but maybe the best reply was penned by Henry David Thoreau in, "Walden" the book he wrote as a record of his own transformational journey at Walden Pond in Massachusetts:

"The mass of men lead lives of quiet desperation. What is called resignation is confirmed desperation. From the desperate city you go into the desperate country, and you have to console yourself with the bravery of minks and muskrats. A stereotyped but unconscious despair

is concealed even under what are called the games and amusements of mankind. There is no play in them, for this comes after work. But it is a characteristic of wisdom not to do desperate things."
- Henry David Thoreau, "Walden" 1854

I love Thoreau's phrase, "... it is a characteristic of wisdom not to do desperate things." Henry David Thoreau was many things, among them an author, poet, philosopher, naturalistic, transcendentalist and maybe known most of all for his moral opposition and civil disobedience in resisting what he believed was an "unjust state." After he woke up from the dream most of us are led to and entranced by, he found a way to walk on a path that was distinctly his own. In waking from the dream that becomes our lives as we know them, Thoreau decided to live a life informed by a manifest wisdom he found within himself and reflected in the world around him ... rather than one organized in desperation.

Now if you do not know what I mean by "the dream," and the difference between that and being "awake," not much of this will make sense to you so far. Let me bring you back for a moment to something I said earlier ... that my own journey began because I was lost. That moment, when I realized I was lost, was the moment when I first recognized that I had been asleep for the past twenty-five years or so. I am giving myself the benefit of the doubt that I made it to the age of five awake when I say twenty-five years. I was following the set of hypnotic commands installed in me and just about everyone I had encountered up until then by the society we lived in together. The suggestions I received as a child, beginning from the moment I was born, continued to deepen and were reinforced by an endless repetition of the same messages coming in from every quarter imaginable. As I stated in my earlier book, **"The State of Perfection: Your Hidden Code to Personal Mastery"** the dominant message of society can be summed up as, **"Be Good and Fit In."**

Even well meaning folks ... my parents, my aunts and uncles, grandparents, teachers, friends (and their parents too) ... were all under the same spell, and installing it in others like a virus. The social virus we are taught to live by in almost any "civilized" culture ... **"Be Good and Fit In"** ... replicates in virtually everyone it touches. The entire system I was raised within was designed and organized to deliver this message, **"Be Good and Fit In."**

INTRODUCTION

The bait to take the poison pill is the prize offered to those who willingly submit ... achievement and success ... beginning with praise lauded on us at the start when we learn to babble out our first few words. The process continues to condition us from before we can think for ourselves to desire the "prize." The conditioning to want to be noticed and well regarded by others continues from our earliest days in school with the gold stars we earn, and the stroking that comes along with them. On the other hand we also learn that when we "fail" we will be summarily punished with a harsh look, a word or more extreme physical intervention or punishment. The least physical punishment is being constrained, from there it may move up the scale to a pat on the behind, and in some instances works up to a significant beating. Worse than physical punishment however, even more than a severe beating that injures us, is banishment ... emotional or literal.

We learn early on to please others, striving at all costs to **"Be Good and Fit In."**

This is the major process we accommodate and absorb during our schooling years to **"Be Good and Fit In."** We learn to remain quiet, not to challenge authority, to do what we're told, to sit still - **ignoring our own body's demands and its pleas that we move and remain free**. We yearn to get the gold star ... the perfect grade in class, the "100%" ... the "A" ... the "4.0" ... and even that's not good enough. We do the extra credit work so we can graduate with better than perfect grades, "110%" ... "A+" ... a "4.3" GPA on a "4.0" scale. Along the way we learn that all we have to do to achieve greatness is to submit to the requests of authority and do what we are told. As a result we learn to do things like blindly submit to the "Rule of Law" as though it is cosmic order and not man-made fabrication ... and for the most part we learn and do our part well. Thoreau's lessons on the obligation of civil disobedience seem to be lost in our generation.

By the time I was thirty years old, I had learned all these lessons well. I had both experienced the reward of doing what I was told and excelling ... and also stepping off the bus and hitting the ground hard. In my case, when I landed no one was there to pick me up. I had one advantage, I was like a pit bull with a bone ... tenacious, reluctant to give up what I held to be mine and a bit pugnacious if I had to be to protect and keep it. That is how I wound up on the stool, eyes closed in profound trance, sitting next to Roye. I knew the beliefs I had accumulated were "real" and that I had to unwind them from my psyche if I ever wanted to be free and have "the experience of my life." I also knew from long experience via trial and error that either I could not or would not do this on my own ... not easily or maybe not at all.

I was on that stool, sitting next to Roye, because I had found a master, and I was about to allow him to guide me over the threshold beyond the edge of reality as I knew it. I was ready, willing and grateful to have found someone to help me to surrender and go "insane."

The rest of this book is a tale of the journey I took into what can only be called utter social insanity, and my return to the world proper, profoundly sane by every measure.

Chapter One:

Stepping Off the Path

"Use what you have."

- Carlo Vinci

CHAPTER ONE

"I Want To Believe ..."

After about ten years in the world of architecture, around the age of 28, I woke up one day and knew it was not for me ... at least not in terms of what I yearned for at the time, i.e.: professional fulfillment and satisfaction. I was like so many of the people I have worked with over the years since then who come to me seeking to find their purpose in life. They presume, as I did, that there is some magical thing they need to be, or should be, doing. We are taught and believe that once we discover our purpose it will allow us to remain in a state of bliss. We believe this because we believe once we find our purpose we will be in some way "cosmically organized" to be doing what we are meant to be doing ... the thing that will fulfill our "divine purpose."

This thinking is part of the New Age dribble that becomes the trite, but catchy, headline some New Age, self-help marketing maven writes to peddle their latest wares like, "Do What You Love and the Money Will Follow" or "The Laws of Abundance" ... or some other such nonsense. Their advice seldom works, but their headlines often do, creating a massive flow of cash for the successful marketer.

Selling a book, or the workshop, or the intensive 21-day retreat at the Canyon Springs Resort or Esalen, isn't the issue in my opinion ... it is the damage that flows from it, i.e.: the book, workshop, retreat ...

Oh, don't get me wrong, the advice makes perfect sense as it is framed in the book, workshop or intensive retreat. The challenge is that it often only works in those rarified contexts, not in the work-a-day world that most of the folks I know and work with actually live in. The promises of everlasting bliss are so tempting, that like FBI Agent Fox Mulder in Chris Carter's "X-Files" ... **"I want to believe."** ...

I can assure you that there is no one, and nothing, that will save you from the desire to believe except yourself ... possibly. To get out of the self-deluding meta-magical thinking trap you will also probably need some help from a knowledgeable "friend" along the way.

What makes me an authority on such things?

Time and again I built up my expectations only to have them sucked into the whirlpool of my false and misleading beliefs, torn to pieces as I tried to navigate my way through the treacherous waters of my personal Charybdis. I thought I was a king in my small kingdom, on a journey to living a good life ... literally on the way to being a good person and living the good life. It was as though I were on a merry-go-round, and all about me gold rings hung waiting to be plucked one after another for my benefit, pleasure and amusement.

I was blessed with a good mind and a good constitution - one of the privileges of coming from good old, salt of the earth, peasant stock. When I applied myself to academics and athletics I excelled. When I decided I needed or wanted to learn something I was able to do so. People naturally seemed to like me and support me. I could be persuasive, and I drew people to myself and my ideas. My business swelled as a result, and I experienced professional and financial success. I found a lovely woman, who fell in love with me, we got married and quickly had a son ... an amazing, beautiful boy who remains so to this day. My own birth family loved me, my parents and brother ... and they loved the new members of my own little growing family too. I was fully accepted and loved by my new wife's family as well. It seemed in that moment I had it all ... not one, but many golden rings in my hands.

Then something exploded in my psyche. I woke up one morning knowing with absolute certainty that I no longer wanted to practice architecture or design. It was not giving me the personal satisfaction or fulfillment I knew I "deserved" as I had been reading about in all the New Age, self-help books littering my shelves. There had to be something more for me out there ... something beyond my current reach ... someone I needed to become. The challenge was I had no idea what that meant or how to go about it.

What I did know is that I needed to act, and act I did. I quit the partnership I was in, finding a way to exit and leave my partners intact. In that decision was the consideration that I would leave with the clothes on my back so to speak, i.e.: no payout from them, although I left with a bit of work to pursue. I spent the next couple of years extricating myself from the sticky mental web I had woven, thinking of myself as an "architect and designer" and all that meant. I tried my hand at running my own solo practice, and while I was successful in getting commissions for work, I remained unfulfilled and unsatisfied. I tried working for a couple of other

CHAPTER ONE

architects, mostly continuing to do interiors work, with no better results. I moved onto the lucrative practice of designing kitchens and baths. I became a de facto partner in a successful kitchen when I became responsible for producing almost half of its total revenue, and the opportunity for partnership was 'gifted' to me. Still, there was no real joy for me.

In the process of "trying to extricate and find myself" I sought out and found a number of self-help, personal development programs ... one of the first was Werner Erhard's EST.

EST is short for "Erhard Seminars Training" and also the Latin for "it is." Werner's program was later renamed, "The Forum," and it is still being presented by Landmark Education worldwide (albeit in a much watered down version from the program I originally attended).

The EST program I attended began with a long, meticulous, tedious recitation of "the rules" which amounted to **"Do what we say, stay in the room, and you'll get 'IT'"** ... the staff presenter summarized by saying, **"If you want 'IT' just keep your sole in the room."**, while touching the bottom of his shoe.

The first thing I remember the official trainer saying at the start of the program was something like,

> *"Do you know why you're here? ...*
>
> ***DO YOU KNOW WHY YOU'RE HERE!!?!???!!! ...***
>
> *Because you're tubes.*
>
> *You put food in one end and live your life waiting for it to come out of the other.*
>
> *You're all assholes and your life doesn't work.*
>
> ***YOU'RE HERE BECAUSE YOUR LIFE DOESN'T WORK!!!!"***

He was standing on a stage a foot or so above the participants seating level, and at the front of the dingy training room, while all the participants looked up at him, slack jawed, from their seats in metal folding chairs, and he went onto ask,

> *"Do you know why I'm up here and you're down there?"*

"I'M UP HERE BECAUSE MY LIFE WORKS, AND YOURS DOESN'T!!!"

He boomed the last bit, literally shouting it at the audience. I soon became inured to the shouting as the weekend progressed, as it was frequent and intense. The trick was either avoiding being the one shouted at, becoming the one being shouted at or some combination of the two depending on your temperament. Since I am a good study I learned my place of comfort rather quickly.

The training was continued over the next weekend, also occupying a night in between the first weekend and the next as well. I loved every minute of it!

At the time I believed that training changed my life, and at some level I still believe it did. At the very least it reset my direction and the course it would take for me. In the final program meeting, after the end of the formal training we were compelled to bring family and friends along, and assist in berating them to sign-up as the starry-eyed converts we had all become ourselves. I left deciding I wanted "more." What I did not quite know was "more" of what it was that I really wanted.

What I did "know" was that what those guys did up there on that stage over those two weekends and two weeknights with the group was what I wanted to do too. I wanted to "train" people, I wanted to be a "trainer" like the fellows I had just experienced being with who were up on stage in front of me.

Although, truth be told, at that time I still did not really know what being a trainer meant … or have the slightest idea regarding how to go about doing it.

Catching The Training Flu

After attending Werner Erhard's EST training, and deciding to become a "trainer" myself, I began by using what I had, a strategy for learning what I wanted to know. The challenge I faced was that I did not know what it would take to become a "trainer" - heck, I did not even know what I did not know about it!

All I had that I could count on was my well honed learning strategy, and I believed I could use it to move to where I wanted to be going.

I wanted to become a "trainer" ... whatever that might mean ... and so I followed my nose. At that point all I had was the profound experience of participating in the EST training and what it looked like from my point of view. So I began to consider what I would need to know to do something like that.

My learning strategy goes back to a much earlier time in my life, early elementary school at least. However, for the purposes of laying out what is most important and leaving out what is not, it is probably best to move things along ... we will jump to the early 1980s when I began an architectural interiors practice with my two partners.

As an architect I was really good at two things:

1. Hiring technical people and training them, and
2. Selling and managing high-end projects, both commercial and residential

In fact I was way better at these two things than I ever was a sitting at a board and drawing myself. I especially liked, and was particularly good at, getting clients to commit working with us on very exclusive projects ... i.e.: sales.

I was a kind of natural born salesperson, if there is such a thing. Once there was someone to sell I liked the whole process of selling. I never loved the prospecting part of sales, the part where you have to drum up someone to sell something to in the first place. Since then I have redefined the idea of the sales process as separate from what I think of as the marketing process, which includes prospecting. Although I would agree they are very closely related, maybe even Siamese twins, sales and marketing retain some distinctions I think of as critical in the way I hold them mentally, and act on them as well.

The marketing process is all about identifying prospects conceptually, then defining an offer they will want to respond to, putting that offer in front of them ... and getting them to identify themselves to you. Doing this as a separate action from what I think of as selling. Some people seem constitutionally organized to do marketing and to do it well … crazy as it seems to me I have even met some people who love marketing.

Selling is not marketing as I see it. The crazy folks I have met who love marketing tell me this is my "problem" with marketing … "Bah, Humbug and Balderdash" to them all! Separating the process of marketing from selling has allowed me to create marketing processes without having to "prospect" in the way some sales people think about it. Just about every sales professional I have ever met or worked with hates the barbaric process of cold calling, where they contact people they don't know, who don't know them, and pitch their wares …

Agggghhhhh!!!! … cold calling … I would rather be Charlie Brown flying through the air as Lucy yanked away the football at the last possible moment.

In life, knowing what is for you, and what is not for you, is one mark of a significant level of self awareness.

Many people do not recognize that they are simply not suited for one thing or another, and endlessly strive to get the thing that does not fit for them right.

Striving to do what is an utter mismatch for you is a very poor choice to make in my opinion. I learned that lesson well, and when I did I could relate it directly to some very bad messages I had received in my upbringing and schooling. Simply stated the message that led me to thinking I should strive to do what did not come naturally to me was, **"Anything worth doing is going to be difficult and take real work."**

Once again, **"Bah, Humbug and Balderdash" to striving!** … especially when it comes to doing what I am not geared up for doing well.

I have nothing against working hard … I work hard all the time when I want something … what I am against is striving. Stuart Wilder, an author whose books I like reading, says that striving is hard work with a negative emotional charge attached to it, and I agree. I actually like working hard … when I enjoy the work. Once I realized the distinction between hard work and striving I had it made in the shade … I could relax, work hard and get on with things from there.

Refusing to "strive" to achieve what I wanted was a major turning point in my life … especially when it came to working professionally. I had learned to notice for what I was naturally good at accomplishing

CHAPTER ONE

effortlessly, even when the work was hard, and I began choosing only to do those things ... and I excelled.

With regard to selling once I had a prospect in front of me I loved the whole dang process that followed. In fact, by following my nose, I stumbled across a way of selling effortlessly and figured something out that made that possible. I would always begin the sales process by asking questions, tons and tons of questions ... about everything. Many of the questions I asked seemed to have little to do with the project we were discussing, or design in even the remotest way, but if a question to ask came to me, I asked it.

I would ask my clients about their lives and have them recite their autobiography to me. Sometimes we would spend hours talking about the foods they like to eat and the restaurants they liked. We would talk about sports and current events, the economy, the political landscape, whatever. Somehow, just by using questions two things emerged that were critical to my success in sales:

> 1) Beginning by talking about things that clients liked and felt good about helped them to access a positive state where the could think clearly for themselves and make good decisions, including ones about buying something.

> 2) Using good questions could lead prospective clients to define what they wanted, and from there they became self-convinced that they should have it.

When I decided to sell something to someone I could be very persuasive. I believe that a lot of it had to do with the fact that I was really, truly interested in what we were talking about, and hearing their answers. Really connecting and finding out how someone "ticked" and what they were interested in made sealing the deal and signing the contract natural and effortless. I became so good at it that I also became committed to making sure they wanted to buy what I was selling, and that they were not buying just not to offend me.

I literally began trying NOT to sell things to clients as a test to make sure they really wanted and would benefit from what they were buying. As naturally as selling came to me, selling ethically in this way came naturally to me as well. Being ethical is incredibly self-servicing, as I found out later on when I began consulting in corporate and organizational settings and with private clients, being ethical served my clients, and saved me untold grief.

Back then I never understood why my clients would let me ask them all the questions I did even though they did not seem to apply to why we had agreed to get together. Then I learned about NLP and rapport. It seems that when you have deep rapport with someone, all the ordinary hesitation to be open disappears, and people begin interacting with you like an old friend. In fact, I had stumbled on a particular way of creating the kind of profound rapport that Roye referred to as "conversationalizing" … and it was mind blowing!

Conversationalizing essentially means that you engage in conversation with someone, as you would with an old friend over coffee, lunch or a few drinks maybe. It often means taking the conversation outside of the expected bounds of the interaction, as I did when I talked about food, restaurants or told stories about myself when I was selling. The added piece of the puzzle that makes what you are doing when you conversationalize is that you act with intention to notice the patterns of interaction that the other person displays, and you follow them yourself. When you do this it builds profound rapport.

Depending on how skillful you are when conversationalizing you can begin by following the topics of conversation they raise … with a bit more skill you follow their movements non-verbally … raise your skillfulness more and you can begin following their language patterns and even their tonal patterns of speech … and when you are masterful you will be able to include seemingly imperceptible things like micro-muscular movements … even to the point of adumbrating what they are about to do and have not done yet, and going there before they do themselves … seeming to read their minds.

Discovering profound rapport fundamentally changed how I interacted with people when I found out about it consciously. Learning about rapport and conversationalizing opened the gates further to something I had originally come across in the EST program I attended:

- **You cannot know what you do not know until after you know about it.**

CHAPTER ONE

- The more you know, the more you begin to know how much you do not know.
- As you learn more, you become aware of what you now know you know nothing about.

When I got the idea that knowing begets knowing it knocked my socks off!

"Hahaha" ... this stuff was priceless.

It became obvious, as you learn the circle of knowledge keeps getting bigger, but as it does at the level where the learning occurs it only serves to illuminate how ignorant we remain at another. For example, quantum physics and relativity enlightened us about the nature of how the Universe works in ways that Newtonian physics never could have for us. At the same time the "New Physics" created many more questions that now need to be answered if we want to understand the deep workings of the Universe. This is especially true compared to how close some physicists thought they might have been to establishing a "Theory of Everything" using purely Newtonian physics.

In the process of thinking about becoming a trainer I began to think about what I needed to know that I did not know yet. I wanted to uncover what I needed to know so that I could learn and begin doing the things that I wanted to do that I could not do yet. For me the connection between knowing and doing had always been clear and evident. I understood that knowledge is most evident in skills, and that skills are most evident in action, and that from action comes experience, and from experience comes more knowledge, e.g.:

>Knowledge >>> Skills
>Skills >>> Action
>Action >>> Experience
>Experience >>> Knowledge

The looping from knowledge through skills and action to experience and back to knowledge is the key to developing mastery.

Knowledge without action was never particularly exciting for me. Once I gathered a critical mass of knowledge I always wanted to test it by doing things. By doing things I discovered the gaps in what I thought I knew or understood, and then I could begin to fill them. Sometimes I would close the gaps between what I thought I knew or understood by refining what I was doing or how I was doing it. The process of taking action generated the new information that filled the gap.

There were times when I just could not figure out where the limitations in the system were on my own and I went "back to the drawing board" ... re-reading books I had already read, talking to the people I had been learning from and finding additional sources of information to expand the way I thought about things. But, before claiming that what I was doing would not work, I would always begin by trying to figure out what was not working for myself first. Choosing to begin from the presumption that things were already working well, and that I just could not see that from the angle or point of view I was observing them from, became a kind of incantation or mantra for me ...

"I can make the things work that seem NOT to be working by noticing what I am already doing that IS working and starting again from there."

With regard to becoming a trainer I knew for sure that I did not know what to do, or how to do the thing called training. What seemed obvious though was that training was a particular way of communicating with people to help them make a change of some kind. At least that is what it seemed like had happened for me in the EST training that was so exciting. In fact the EST folks even mentioned that it was all about creating a change in the way we thought and communicated. Based on that assessment of what the trainers had done I began to look towards getting some information about how people think and communicate that creates meaningful, positive change in their lives.

I took some Master's level university courses in cognitive neuroscience hoping they might provide some answers about how people think , communicate and make changes. Par for the course, the coursework was fascinating to me, pursuing the Master's degree was not. Somehow as I was doing this I had gotten on a mailing list and received a brochure from the New York Training Institute for NLP. I read the brochure and it sounded perfect, a training that lead up to a Trainer's Certification in what sounded to me like cutting edge neuroscientific sounding stuff about helping people change the way they thought and communicated. I was sold before I was done looking over the brochure.

I called the New York Training Institute for NLP and spoke to someone there with the intention of signing up for their NLP Practitioner certification training program. I figured that with what I would learn in the program I could begin to start working with people to help them to make changes they wanted to make in their lives or businesses. However, whomever I spoke with on the phone that day just did not resonate with me, so I gave up on attending that training program. Coincidentally, and serendipitously, I found a brochure in a health food store a short time afterwards for an NLP Practitioner certification training program from another institute based in New Jersey. I called the number on the brochure, spoke with the person who answered, and signed up for the program then and there. Not only am I a good salesperson, but I am also really easy to sell to when I want to buy something … and I was in a buying mode that day.

Finally, I was on my way to becoming a trainer.

Going To The Dogs

It seemed fortuitous that I found the brochure and signed up for the NLP Practitioner Certification Training program offered by the institute in New Jersey just before it was about to begin. The program was a perfect fit for my interests and needs at the time.

When I get something stuck in my head I am on it and typically I do not … or maybe more accurately said, I will not … let it go. Once I "discovered" NLP I was convinced that it was the route I needed to take, and I was dead set on making it happen. So within a couple of weeks of first coming across NLP, and days after I had picked up the brochure for the Practitioner Certification Training program, I was in a room with a bunch of folks I did not yet know learning all about neurolinguistic programming.

At the same time as I was attending the NLP Practitioner Certification Training program I returned to training dogs, something I had done in my teens. I always loved dogs and got along with them naturally. By the age of eight or nine I could name every registered breed with the American Kennel Club on sight, and usually knew a bit about them as well, e.g.: what "group" were they registered in, Working Dogs, Hounds, Terriers, etc. ... so I was kind of a "natural" by the time I was a teenager, having already probably put in more than 10,000 hours of work reading, observing and trying my hand at training. I convinced a local professional dog trainer, who had been a K-9 handler in the military before opening a civilian training company, to give me a shot at working with him. He sent me out on a trial training job, got a good report from the dog owners, and hired me. I continued to train dogs while I was playing at going to college, and I learned a lot about how to do it well, and also about the business. So when the time came around again to filling the coffers, while I was trying to "find myself," dog training was an automatic answer for me.

    About a year and a half earlier, around the time my son was born, I met a fellow who was a master dog trainer himself, a gent named Bob Brandau. Bob is a genius with dogs, and a total character everywhere else in his life. With a leash in his hand, or just as often wrapped around his waist, and working with a dog off-leash, he can do things that would rival David Copperfield on stage in Las Vegas. Maybe comparing Bob when he's training dogs to Mr. Spock from Star Trek would be more correct ... he seems able to "mind-meld" with the dogs he works with telepathically. He walks into a room and the dogs start paying attention to him, obeying every request he makes of them. When Bob is working with a dog it looks like magic, and when I saw it I wanted to have that skill too.

    So I persuaded Bob to train me to train dogs. I went up at the urging of a common friend, I man I had met when I bought my first wife a dog, a Doberman Pinscher, she named "Ninja" ... a great "little" dog (she was really little for a Doberman). He had bought his brood bitch, "Kessey," from Bob. She was an AKC breed champion, and a Schutzhund champion as well (NOTE: Schutzhund are protection dog trials and a certification that began in Germany). We went up to Bob's place and when we got there he was training a pit bull, "Flash," who was being handled by his owner, a young girl named Julie. Bob was doing what is known in protection dog training as "agitation" ... or impelling the dog to become aggressive towards an agitator filling in for a 'bad guy."

    The intention of doing agitation with a dog is to train it to bite, while it remains in the control of the handler. After I was introduced to

CHAPTER ONE

Bob, and I expressed an interest in learning from him, he said, "I don't do students, sorry." Then he asked if I would like to try my hand at agitating the pit bull he was working with anyway, and I said, "Sure." Up until that point I had only done military type agitation and some Shutzhund type training, so I went at it as I knew how. I came at the dog, agitated it, offered it the bite on a protection sleeve I was wearing, basically a burlap covered leather and plastic tube that covers the agitator's arm and prevents you from actually getting bitten.

The dog took the bite and I began to "calm the dog in the bite" as I had learned to do before. This meant stroking the dog under its chin as it was biting down on the sleeve, with the stick in my opposite hand. Immediately this dog let go of the sleeve and promptly bit the hand that was stroking it. Once we got Julie to get Flash to open his mouth and let go of my hand we could see that the bite was minimal but significant. Flash had only gotten one canine into my palm, but it had gone through to meet the canine on the other side, so I had a hole in my hand. Bob brought me into his house, got some antiseptic cream, some bandages and some tape. I washed the hand off thoroughly, poured some of the hydrogen peroxide he had also brought with him into the wound, and at that point saw some bits and pieces sticking out. I asked Bob for a sharp scissors and cut them off. The I packed the wound, bandaged and taped it, and told Bob that we should go back out and give Flash a good bite, because we did not want to leave him with a bad bite for the day.

Bob just looked at me, his lips parted a bit, and said, "Okay, ... are you sure?" I said that I was and we went back out. We worked a bit more agitating Flash, and finished up the day. Bob then asked me if I would like to come up again, I replied that I would and that was that. I became Bob's apprentice (a pattern in my learning style), I walked a lot of dogs, cleaned a lot of cages and learned a tremendous amount of what it really means to train a dog. Along the way Bob and I built a lasting mutual respect for one another, and a close friendship, that continues to this day.

With Bob, learning was all about "being present" ... literally like a Renaissance or Guild type apprenticeship, the master allowed me to hang around and pick up what I could. When I had begun to get something he would extend the learning via trial by fire and give me a task to do. I would do the best I could with what I had picked up from watching him working with dogs and trying things out on my own, and then he would come down on me like a sledgehammer pointing out the things I needed to adjust. This process was repeated again and again, repetition after repetition, until I mastered that aspect of what I was learning. It was like what the Werner Erhard folks had said, **"Keep your sole in the room and you'll get it."**

This was the real thing as far as I was concerned ... learning by example and immersion, trial by fire, repetition and refinement ... I was in learning heaven!

Truth be told, Bob has always been a better dog trainer than I will ever be - but, where he innately excelled at training dogs I innately excelled at unpacking information and making it explicit. I found out from his "teaching style" that he actually did not know the first thing about how to teach what he knew. In fact as often as not he was trying to teach me something that was exactly the opposite of what he himself was doing. So I stopped paying attention to what he told me to do, and started paying strict attention to what he did ... then I taught him what he did instead of what he said he was doing. Afterwards he would confirm if what I thought he was doing was correct or not and we would adjust it until it was just right. Little by little in this way I accumulated the knowledge and skills I hoped to gain from him.

From what Bob taught me, and in the process teaching him about how to teach what it was he knew, I had become pretty darn masterful working with the dogs. I reached a point where I knew without a doubt I could train a dog, or "walk a dog" as Bob liked to say, and I began to consider the commonalities with the "training" I had experienced in the EST program ... and what that might suggest. One of the things that stood out for me was that most of the "dog training" I was doing had much more to do with training the people that owned them, than the dogs I was hired to "train" - and I also knew I loved the work I was doing. I felt in that moment like I might be onto something.

While I was apprenticing with Bob, learning to train dogs, I remained deep in the process of learning NLP as well. I was reading every book on NLP I could get my hands on. During that year I was also in the year long NLP Practitioner Certification Training program meeting for one weekend a month with the New Jersey based NLP trainers. On the training weekends I was repeatedly amazed by what we were learning. I kept seeing parallels to dog training, and I remember thinking that it seemed at times there was more talking going on than any demonstration, application or practice. It was very unlike how I was learning with Bob.

CHAPTER ONE

About midway during that year I met Richard Bandler, one of the co-developers of the original NLP model, when the folks running the training invited him to spend an evening with us. Like Bob was magical with the dogs, Richard was a magician in working with people and he demonstrated everything I thought and hoped this NLP "stuff" would be. That night, I decided I would learn what Richard was doing and how he did it, become an NLP trainer myself, and do that for the rest of my life.

Somewhere along the way, between quitting my design career, pursuing personal development training, re-starting my dog training career and beginning to learn NLP, my marriage came to its end and I was back "home" living with my parents ... again.

By now it was clear that I had stepped pretty far off the path I had been raised to run on ... i.e.: "go to school, get good grades, get a good job, get married, raise a family" - the standard, **"Be Good and Fit In."**

Somewhat unbidden, "Adventure" called and I had answered loud and clear ... "I'm in!"

Author's Note: *It was right around this time in my life that I first met Roye - however, before jumping there I will digress a bit to set the stage for the significance of that meeting and give you a bit of background before coming back again to that part of the story.*

Chapter Two:

Answering the Call

"Lions and Tigers and Bears ... Oh my."
- Dorothy in the "Wizard of Oz"

CHAPTER THREE

Crossing The Threshold

One of my intellectual mentors was the scholar and renowned mythologist, Joseph Campbell. While I never met Joseph Campbell, I have been highly influenced by him and his work. His model of human development, "The Hero's Journey" has been one of the most significant influences on me as a professional, and on the development of the model I have been working on for more than two decades, the MythoSelf Process model.

I first came across Joseph Campbell's "Hero's Journey" in his book, "The Hero With a Thousand Faces" first published in 1934. The "Hero's Journey" is essentially a map of what he calls, becoming human. It is the universal experience of the hero as told in myths and stories around the world from time immemorial. This story always begins the same way, with a "Call to Adventure."

At the start of the story the would-be hero is living their life 'normally' ... he or she fits in to the context they were born into and they are doing everything they can to 'fit in and be good' as is expected of them. Often they achieve some degree of success in this way, sometimes significant success. Some of these stories even start with the a hero that is royal born, someone on the path to becoming a King or a Queen. This is the case of the famous story of the first Buddha, Siddhartha Guatama who was a Prince in a province of ancient Nepal or India, destined one day to become King.

In the Buddha's case he was living a sheltered life designed by his father, the King. His father was a great Hindu warrior and leader, a great conqueror who desperately wanted his son to follow him and rule the kingdom he had created. Upon the birth of his son a renowned Hindu seer, a fortune-teller of sorts, forecast that the baby, Siddhartha, would either be a great ruler or a great holy man ... a prophet. Siddhartha's father, King Suddhodana, wanted to insure that Siddhartha would become the king.

To prevent the future Buddha from becoming a holy man or a prophet he insulated him from the world outside the palace and the external suffering present there. Within the walls of the palace Siddhartha only knew youthfulness, health, comfort and joy. He was raised never having encountered sickness or death. At a young age he was married to a distant cousin, who it is said quickly gave birth to a son. For twenty-nine years Siddhartha remained behind the palace walls. The only life he imagined was the one he was living, and the future expectation of becoming a warrior king himself someday.

Upon reaching his twenty-ninth birthday Siddhartha, the future Buddha, went out to meet his people*. Along the way he saw an old man and was stunned by his appearance. Asking his retainer what this was, he was told it was old age. Further along on this journey he saw a dead corpse being wrapped and taken away, again he was stunned. He asked, "What is this?", and was told it was death. Up until that moment Siddhartha had not known of death. In that moment he was transformed. The world he knew and counted on had just evaporated. In its place a new one instantly formed, a world with old age, death and suffering. In that moment Siddhartha was released from his old life as he knew it and was called to another. His old life was utterly dead to him, as were his parents and all his relations - including family and friends - as he knew them. He had figuratively killed his parents, and in so doing Siddhartha killed their dreams and expectations of the life he should and would lead ... and was on his way to becoming Guatama Buddha.

This is an example of being called to Adventure as Joseph Campbell puts it. You're living your life comfortably, your expectations are in place and make sense to you ... the world, and your life in it, are unfolding as they should ... and then, BAM! ... something unexpected happens. From the sense of knowing who you are, how the world works and your place in it, you are shaken to find out it isn't that way at all. There's more to the world and your life in it than you could ever have known or conceived of on your own. I call this experience "getting the itch" ... getting it is like getting bitten by a mosquito and needing to scratch to relieve the discomfort. For most people this is how the Adventure comes, without warning that the cozy, comfortable, secure life they thought they were building isn't so cozy, comfortable or secure as they had thought.

Campbell says that when the Call to Adventure strikes a person it can come in one of two ways. Either the would-be hero can respond to the call and seek the life they are being called to as Siddhartha did, or they can reject the call and return to the life as they knew it to be and hope it

CHAPTER THREE

remains that way. Of course after hearing the Call to Adventure they can never really go back. Prior to hearing the Call their life as they knew it to be was not just all they knew, it was literally all there was from their point of view. When most people first encounter the Call to Adventure life as they know it is not limited to the life they are living, it represents the totality of what life could be ... period, full stop ... the whole enchilada "as is" without exception. After the Call they know with certainty that the life they had been living was a carefully constructed and orchestrated lie designed to point them in a direction, and keep them pointed that way.

When the original certainty is lost ... the certainty that the world and life is how you were told they would be ... you come to know the world, life and yourself differently, and you can never return to the original innocence you once possessed unscathed. Those who turn away from adventure often do so by becoming orthodox about their beliefs, rituals and traditions in the way they held them as a child, and that in turn held them too. Another option when rejecting the adventure would be to find new beliefs, rituals and traditions to latch onto to keep the world from spinning out of control. Regardless of how they might try to return to the old world ... the one they counted on, the one they supposed would continue to give them security in how things are and will be ... they know they are lost. The world they knew and believed in doesn't exist for them anymore ... and the itch they now have never truly goes away.

Joseph Campbell said that the Adventure not taken ... or in my words, "the itch not scratched" ... becomes a crisis for the person who has rejected and denied it. The Call will come again, but the next time more urgently than the last. If a person continues to avoid it, the Call to Adventure eventually becomes a full-blown crisis, exploding their world into pieces with some kind of calamity or tragedy. The calamity or tragedy that tears the hero's world apart could be an accident, sickness they experience themselves or the death of someone they love. The crisis can come as the loss of something precious, e.g.: one's marriage, career or reputation. It can show up as a physical, emotional, mental, social or spiritual breakdown. One way or another the Call to Adventure will press itself into the life of the hero and demand a response.

Chapter Two – Crossing The Threshold Notes:

*It is interesting to note that there seems to be a pattern in the spiritual traditions of becoming aware, or awakening, at around or after the age of thirty or so. The Buddha began his awakening upon seeing suffering, disease and death at the age of 29, and began teaching around the age of 35. In the Christian bible Jesus is also said to have begun his ministry at around the age of thirty. The Prophet Muhammad began visiting a cave on Mt. Hira outside of Mecca in his thirties and at the age of forty was visited there by the Archangel Gabriel and began his ministry.

In addition to the pattern in some spiritual traditions of the great teachers becoming aware or awakening at around or after the age of thirty or so, there is also another pattern of them rejecting their past and those closest to them as the Buddha had done, as well as being rejected by this closest to them.

We see this pattern documented in many spiritual texts, like the Judeo-Christian bible's comments about prophets:

"A prophet is not without honor, but in his own country, and among his own kin, and in his own house." - KJV Bible, Mark 6:4

The story of rejection is told again and again in the great religions of the world, the Buddha rejecting his family and his family rejecting his "holy wandering" as he turns his back to them ... in Judaic teaching Moses is also seen as being rejected at numerous times during his role as a prophet ... and the story of Jesus Christ in the Christian tradition is one of turning away as well:

> He said to another man, *"Follow me."*
> But the man replied, *"Lord, first let me go and bury my father."*
> Jesus said to him, *"Let the dead bury their own dead, but you go and proclaim the kingdom of God."*
> Still another said, *"I will follow you, Lord; but first let me go back and say good bye to my family."*
> Jesus replied, *"No one who puts his hand to the plow and looks back is fit for service in the kingdom of God."*
> -NIV Bible, Luke 9:59-62

Large crowds were traveling with Jesus, and turning to them he said:

CHAPTER THREE

> *"If anyone comes to me and does not hate father and mother, wife and children, brothers and sisters—yes, even their own life—such a person cannot be my disciple. And whoever does not carry their cross and follow me cannot be my disciple."*
> - NIV Bible Luke 14:25-27

and in turn the great teachers were rejected by those closest to them ...

> *"Truly I tell you,"* he continued, *"no prophet is accepted in his hometown. I assure you that there were many widows in Israel in Elijah's time, when the sky was shut for three and a half years and there was a severe famine throughout the land. Yet Elijah was not sent to any of them, but to a widow in Zarephath in the region of Sidon. And there were many in Israel with leprosy in the time of Elisha the prophet, yet not one of them was cleansed—only Naaman the Syrian."*
>
> *"All the people in the synagogue were furious when they heard this. They got up, drove him out of the town, and took him to the brow of the hill on which the town was built, in order to throw him off the cliff. But he walked right through the crowd and went on his way."*
> - NIV Bible, Luke 4:24 - 30

In a similar way at the beginning of his ministry the Prophet Muhammad's teaching was rejected by many he confided in, and it took him four years to gather just forty followers. Although some of his family and friends accepted his message, including his wife and adopted son, some of those closest to him, such as his own uncle Abu Lahab, fiercely rejected the Prophet Muhammad and his teaching.

Despite the initial rejection in their own lands and during their own time, the great prophets and teachers still built large followings and changed the course of human history. The messages they shared, as well as the messages contained in their lives, continues to resonate through time long beyond the time allotted to them among the living.

Confronting The Crisis

In my case it felt like all of the things that could signal crisis were colliding and creating a perfect storm in what was recently my cozy, comfortable life. At the age of 28 going on 29, I was lost. I thought I had it all, and in the course of a year I found out that it was all a mirage ... a house of cards built on a foundation of sand. I was in what I thought of as "existential" crisis, the need and desire to find meaning. I believed at the time I was being called to do something, to find my golden path, to discover my purpose ... and that maybe even some kind of greatness awaited me. I was wrong.

I was in "ontological" crisis, I urgently needed to know who I was ... and who I was becoming. The ontological longing was insatiable, like thirst in the desert. At the time I would have, and did, give up anything and everything for *"uisce beatha"* as it is called in Gaelic, or "the water of life" in English. I had little but the hope that I would discover something that would quench my desire for salvation. The thirst was unbearable causing me to writhe in anguish at everything I attempted to do, save one thing. I was trying desperately to cling to what I knew, to hang onto the known to get back to what I had ... my marriage and son, my work, my success ... my life as I knew it to be, all to absolutely no avail.

I had to move on, I literally had no choice. There was nothing to go back to, and there was no one who would have wanted me if I did try to go back, especially as I was changing and beginning to become someone else. Maybe I could have gone back if I could have found a way to return to who I had been. I had no way to do that, and truth be told, no desire to if I could ... I had already gone too far for that to remain an option for me. The only way out was forward. So I began plowing onwards ... or should I say downward?

It was evident to me early on in my crisis that I had built my life on a foundation of sand, nothing was steady, nothing could stand the way I had done things. Somehow instinctively I knew that I had to go down deeper, right where I was standing, to find the bedrock ... the core of my life. I was convinced if I could do that, I could find what I had become desperate for and begin rebuilding a life on a sound and solid footing.

The place to begin was right where I was standing. To progress I had to dig in and commit ... so I did. I went back to my independent scholar ways, reading everything I could get my hands on about what I thought was happening to me. In the process I consumed enormous amounts of spiritual literature, philosophy, science, anthropology, sociology, psychology, fiction as well as a lot of New Age junk, with a couple of New Age gems thrown in for good measure too.

CHAPTER THREE

For what it is worth, much of what I was reading was not new to me. There were books I had read years before that gave me the basis for the work I was now doing. As an adolescent I had become enamored with the Asian Martial Arts, first Karate and then Jujitsu, and later on Aikido (or more accurately, Aiki-Jujitsu). I read as much as I could about Bushido, the Japanese warriors way. As a result of my interest in martial arts I began reading some of the Eastern Philosophical classics, many from the Taoist and Zen canon. This lead me to other things, like some of the American Transcendentalists and Pragmatists. That reading in turn somehow led me to the works of four of the most influential fiction authors in my life - J.R. Tolkien's "The "Hobbit" ... J. W. Norwood's book "The Judoka" ... Carlos Castaneda's "Don Juan" series ... and Frank Herbert's "Dune" science-fiction/fantasy series. As much as any book or author had done or would do these four writers influenced me when I first met them years before ... or they at least helped to set the stage for the change I was experiencing to happen as it now was unfolding.

I revisited some of my "old friends" on the shelf at this time, folks like Alan Watts the great orientalist-philosopher-priest, Thomas Merton the Trappist Monk caught in a Taoist/Zen web, Joseph Chilton Pearce the doctor who had become a New Age guru of sorts, David Bohm the philosopher-physicist and of course the great mythologist, Joseph Campbell ... among others. I also began reaching out and finding some new "friends" ... Richard Bandler and John Grinder, the co-developers of NLP, became popular references for me. From NLP I found the communication theorists and cyberneticists Gregory Bateson and Paul Watzlawick, and folks working with applied communication theory like the famed medical hypnotist Milton H. Erickson and his apprentice Earnest Rossi. I also began reading the existentialist philosophers more deeply. e.g.: Soren Kirkegaard and Martin Heidegger, and the analytic philosophers Ludwig Wittgenstein and John Searle. These were some of the folks influencing me in those early years of my ontological quest. But the most important player in my journey was yet to come.

There were two anchors holding me fast, preventing me from spinning out of control and plunging down to unbearable depths of despair, despite my ontological longing and the crisis it provoked. There were three things I could count on at the time of my crisis - the mastery I was pursuing as a dog trainer, my study of NLP and my commitment to my toddler son. The year I was attending my first NLP Practitioner training was rapidly coming to an end, and I knew I wanted to continue. I knew there was much, much more for me to learn and I wanted to learn it all. I just did not necessarily want to continue learning with the same two trainers with whom I had begun my studies of NLP. They were good, as was the team they had created around them, but I had experienced magic the night that Richard Bandler took the group for a ride beyond the obvious.

I wanted more of that magic, so I began looking for a magician.

I searched and found a number of NLP trainers who were doing training, and I went to programs they were running. I met a number of well-known hypnotists who were running hypnosis training programs, and I went to those as well. I also sought out other possible paths to further my quest, thinking at the time, **"The only way out is forward."** Although I met many skilled and skillful teachers I had not come across a magician yet …

"Toto, I've A Feeling We're Not In Kansas Anymore."

One day I was reading a New Age advertising journal and I saw an ad for a local NLP Master Trainer who was running training programs relatively near to where I was living in N.J. The trainer's name was Roye Fraser. The ad he ran had the headline "Stalking Reality" and there was a quote praising Roye written by Richard Bandler below it. The only other thing I remember was that there was a phone number to call. I read the ad, saw the number to call, and I did. A woman named "Linda" answered, and I asked her about the program advertised in the ad. During the call Linda kept repeatedly telling me, "You just have to come!"

After speaking with Linda I gave in and signed up for a three day program called, "The Generative Imprint" that I understood was based on or around NLP. I got the details about attending the training program from what Linda was saying in between "You just have to come!" … and all I knew for sure about the program was that I could not afford it. Literally, I did not have the money when I said I would come, and I did not know where to get it either.

CHAPTER THREE

I went to where I was told the training was taking place in Pemberton, N.J. on the edge of the New Jersey Pine Barrens. The Pine Barrens are a primeval coniferous swampland, and it is said that some places within the Pine Barrens have not felt human footfalls for more than 10,000 years. I drove from where I was living with my parents in northeast New Jersey about two hours south, into the center of the state, to the Blue Dell Farm, where Roye was running his training programs. Although I followed the directions given to me I simply could not find the Blue Dell Farm. I drove up and down on the road where I thought the "training center" had to be, but there was no training center to be found.

Finally, after making two or three passes, I noticed a mail box with an address and a small sign that said, "Blue Dell Farm," and I pulled into the driveway next to it. The driveway was bounded by tall hedges and trees, and I could not see a thing beyond them from the road. A house appeared on my right as I pulled into the drive. A bit further on the driveway led to an open clearing of sorts where cars were parked, so I pulled up to an empty space, parked and got out of my car. I walked to the house, found the entrance and rang the doorbell. Someone answered and I asked about the training program. They pointed me to a cinderblock building on the other side of the clearing.

I thanked the person who had answered the door, walked across to the building that was pointed out to me, found an open door, and walked in. The door led into a small room where a bunch of people were milling about talking with one another. I looked for Linda or Roye, but I had no idea who they were, or what they looked like. When I asked someone they introduced me to Linda, and she told me Roye was not in the room yet. There was coffee, tea and some biscuits that people were snacking on, so I poured a coffee and waited.

After I had my coffee someone indicated that the training would take place in a larger room off the smaller one I had entered. Another door connected the small room to a larger one, and we went through it into the "Hypnotorium" as I was to find out it was called. The room had been an old mechanic's garage on the property that Roye converted into a training room. There were windows all around letting in plenty of natural light. The room was nicely set up with soft comfortable chairs and couches, big pillows on the floor, and a counter with two stools at the front of the room. The whole thing had a really funky feel to it, like a cross between what I imagine someone's living room in a kibbutz might be like and an upscale modern grunge boutique hotel lounge. At the back there was a small table, and in one corner there was another door leading to a toilet that I had not noticed at first. Attached to the larger room was a small alcove, with two sliding doors leading to the property outside.

The group was friendly, and I began to hear stories about why they were there and about their experiences with Roye. The general theme that emerged sounded surprisingly layered to my ears. In the NLP training I had previously attended everyone was there to learn NLP and to get certified ... or they were there as part of the training team. In the Hypnotorium there were some folks wanting to get certified as NLP Practitioners or Master Practitioners as I did at the time, but most were more interested in their personal development than in becoming trained or certified in NLP. I found out that these folks were primarily there because they had come to Roye to address some issue in their life.

Many of the people I met that first day in the Hypnotorium had some kind of relationship issue ... either personal and intimate ... with a spouse, a partner or a lover, because they had just broken up with someone, gotten separated or divorced ... or because they were not in a relationship and wanted to be in one.

Some people in the room had relationship issues with their children, their parents or both. There were other folks in the room who needed to reset themselves to move on, maybe to further their careers ... and there were those who were in a position to leap forward and wanted some guidance on how to manage themselves and the leap they were about to take. One or two people were there because they were just stuck, period ... their lives were not working as they hoped for one reason or another. A couple of them were convinced that health issues they were experiencing were manifestations of something that remained unfulfilled for them and they wanted to break free of the pattern that was causing it. And of course, there were the ones, who like me, were focused on learning NLP. I felt strangely comforted by all these "misfits" surrounding me. I knew why I was there ... to continue studying for my NLP Master Practitioner's certification, none of this wacky self-help stuff for me ... no, No, NO!

That first morning, as things were just beginning, I was sitting in a chair facing some people on a couch opposite me engaged in some casual conversation. At one point I could feel the room around me change ... like someone had sucked all the old air out and replaced it with

CHAPTER THREE

pure oxygen. I shifted my position in the chair slightly so I could better see the entrance. A man with big bushy white eyebrows and an amazing shock of white hair peeping out from under a black beret had walked in and was moving across the room towards where I was sitting. As he did he greeted a number of people with a Cheshire Cat grin, and the folks he was greeting broke out in big, old smiles themselves. It was Roye. As best as I can remember it, Roye was wearing a pair of black shorts, a black and white silk shirt with swirling patterns on it and open leather sandals. His attire was totally appropriate for the summertime climate in New Jersey … excluding the black beret he was wearing over that unruly white mane of his. The whole image he created struck me as odd, unusual or maybe eccentric for some inexplicable reason though.

I was captured by the feeling I was somewhere truly unique and that something profound was about to happen. The closest I can come to describing what I was feeling would be what I imagine Dorothy felt when she arrived in Oz. Dorothy knew with absolute certainty that she was not in Kansas anymore when the lion blocked her path on the way to visit the wizard … simultaneously paralyzing her for a moment or two, and forcing her to confront him … both out of fear and indignation.

Chapter Three:

A New Way of Learning

"Hokey religions and ancient weapons are no match for a good blaster at your side, kid."
- Han Solo
Star Wars Episode IV: A New Hope

CHAPTER THREE

Interstellar Zen Tales

One of the things I have come to believe as I stepped into and began living my own journey is that story is the natural language of the human mind. Stories connect us to our deepest longings and our deepest knowing. I will go so far as to suggest that we are literally designed to think in the form of stories. We organize our sense of identity, meaning, purpose and destiny in a specific kind of story ... our autobiographical narrative.

Autobiographical narratives are organized like all mythological stories, i.e.: in mythic form. Mythological stories fit a kind of natural lock and key system within us so they go deeply into our psyches, open us up in some way and reveal something important to us. Sometimes myths are stories about how the Cosmos works, e.g.: the natural order of things, as in how we experience time unfolding sequentially, but not necessarily linearly. Closer to home, a second type of myth tell us about how the world around us works and how we can fit into it ourselves, e.g.: these are like our stories about our national or familial identities, where we come from and who we are in relation to others - including how to behave and interact with them.

A third kind of story that shares mythic form points us towards the miraculous, and nudges us to become deeply, profoundly aware of our lives and the wonder contained within them. These are the stories about that which we do not or cannot know ... the mysteries of the Universe. The stories of wonder can be fantastical, tugging relentlessly at the imagination like works of great science fiction, and others are more about the unfolding of wonder that sometimes exceeds the fantasy of science fiction, like Albert Einstein's revelations about space, time and Relativity.

A fourth kind of mythic story reveals us to ourselves. There are myths that point the way within; they are the maps of inner space. While many kinds of stories depend on external evidence to shape and provide them with form, the myths of inner space only make sense in relation to who we know ourselves to be ... and who we are longing to become.

I always felt this way about the story told in the movie "The Wizard of Oz." We all contain a bit of the Scarecrow, Tin Man and Lion from that story. We all also seek the Great Wizard who will complete what we experience as missing from our being, while knowing that such a wonder can in reality only be a sham.

Even as a child I somehow intuited while watching the "Wizard of Oz" that we must somehow complete ourselves. We achieve becoming complete by choosing to live our lives fully; learning along the way as we confront the challenges, trials, demons and monsters on our journey. In learning who we truly are we must make peace with whatever we find as we do, despite the flaws and foibles we discover. This process of uncovering the myth that informs us at our core is as much the Quixotic Quest as the Hero's Journey. Most of all we learn how we are living the myth of Dorothy, desperately seeking a way back "home" … while possessing the key to our own redemption within ourselves.

George Lucas' 1977 film "Star Wars" resonated in me in much the same way for me as a teenager as the "Wizard of Oz" did for me as a child … hinting at both a longing and a knowing that was just beyond my reach, when as a 17 year old adolescent I first encountered it. In the film we are introduced to one of the main characters early on, Luke Skywalker. Luke is the personification of Joseph Campbell's "Hero." Almost immediately, Campbell's map of the "Hero's Journey" begins unfolding as Luke is first introduced.

Luke is living an "ordinary" life, but he holds a dream about Adventure … specifically about becoming a Starfighter pilot for the Rebellion. Yet he is held back, his uncle needs him on the farm for "one more year." However, the Call of Adventure is looming, he has heard it loud and clear … and he has rejected it in favor of satisfying his uncle's request. What he, and we as the viewers, do not yet know is that crisis is also looming, right around the corner. This is the main thing about the Adventure, it will not be denied.

In the Star Wars story just a short while after Luke promised his uncle that he would stay another year on the farm disaster and crisis strike. Luke goes off to retrieve an errant droid that went to deliver a message to "Old Ben Kenobe" a recluse of sorts that is known to Luke. Unknown to him at the time, the man Luke knows as Old Ben Kenobe is really Obi Wan Kenobe, a Jedi Knight. A series of events follow quickly on the heels of Luke meeting Obi Wan, including the death of Luke's

CHAPTER THREE

substitute parents, his aunt and uncle, and the destruction of his home. Part of mythic form is that the hero must kill their parents, or at least the parent of the same gender. If the Hero does not kill his or her parents they will be killed in the story in some way, often preemptively, releasing them from living their parent's story. Only after the parent is dead can the hero can get on with their life and begin creating their own story. Due to the series of events that unfold, Luke has no one, and no home, to return to … and he must venture out into the world on his own. This is a common mythological theme.

Soon Luke and Obi Wan Kenobe find themselves in an interstellar bar, "Chalmun's Cantina" in the pirate city of Mos Eisley on the same planet that Luke is from, Tatooine. The scene is mind-boggling, with the most diverse and varied assortment of extraterrestrials ever assembled in one place at one time. Music is blaring, as it should in a pirate bar, and there is the threat of violence and danger lurking in every corner. It does not take Luke long to find himself confronted and under attack. He is about to die violently when Obi Wan Kenobe saves him with a violent response of his own. What is interesting is how matter-of-factly Obi Wan responds, and how equally banally it is accepted by the cantina's patrons. We have to accept that this is not the ordinary world as we know it, and suspend our disbelief for the time being, if we want to continue experiencing Luke's story.

Clearly, Luke has crossed the threshold of Adventure as Joseph Campbell tells us about it. Crossing the threshold takes some doing, and is inevitable for all would-be heroes. Once the threshold is crossed it is impossible to return to one's "ordinary" life. Crossing the threshold requires one to have what Campbell refers to as a Guide, someone who has been there before to lead and assist you in managing the crossing. In the Star Wars scene with Luke and Obi Wan Kenobe at the cantina we are watching a Guide (Obi Wan Kenobi) lead a would-be Hero (Luke Skywalker) to the threshold, and from there into the Adventure.

The moment of crossing has an air of absolute risk and danger about it. Once over the threshold, the Hero is on the Adventure … they are outside of their ordinary world and their ordinary comfort zone, and maybe in way over their heads. This was most definitely the experience I had on my first day sitting there in the Hypnotorium that Roye built …

I was no longer in the world,
I was out of my comfort zone ... and in way over my head.

As he walked toward me I could see that Roye was kind of tall, maybe six feet or so, and kind of heavy set ... not fat, but solid. He appeared to me like a big man, substantial, but also graceful ... light on his feet and sure of his movements. I had met guys like this in the boxing ring, on the wrestling mat, and in the dojos I had spend hours and hours in over the years. He was literally smiling ear to ear, and I noticed for the first time he had a cigarette he was smoking. The combination of everything going on was disconcerting. On one hand he looked like a kindly grandfather, with his shock of white hair, big bushy, white eyebrows, that Cheshire Cat smile he was wearing. While he was friendly with folks in the room, jauntering about, he also appeared dangerous, like a predator ... I had the immediate impression that I was held in the gaze of a jungle cat.

When he approached me he held out his hand and said something like,"*Ah, what do we have here, fresh meat.*" It was not a question, it was a statement ... one that went a long way in confirming my assessment associating him with a predatory jungle cat. I realized then and there that I was the only one in the room who was new to this forum ... a "newbie" to the Hypnotorium, and the world of Roye Fraser.

He remained relaxed, looking comfortable and at ease, while I felt like a mouse in a trap, or with a cat's paw on my tail holding me in place ... or maybe it was worse than that and the paw was on my neck . He introduced himself and asked, "So what do you know about?" The room had shifted imperceptibly and by the time I noticed it everyone had moved into a circle around us, and they were watching and listening. I knew what was happening was a test of some kind. Remembering when I wanted to be I could be a good student, so I thought before I spoke, carefully choosing my response, and I said, "**I know about Zen.**" - a topic I was pretty secure in talking about then.

Roye tilted his head back a fraction and laughed. I did not think about it in that moment, but in retrospect he was like a totally secure predator offering me a chance at his throat, making himself a bit vulnerable. It was as though he were subtly challenging me, and showing me he had nothing to be concerned with from me at the same time. He

CHAPTER THREE

could afford to show me his soft spot and there was not a thing I could do about it. It was a masterful stroke of non-verbal dueling, positioning himself as dominant in the relationship, and quelling any fight before it could begin ... **Fuck me!!!**

Roye then said, "*Okay tell me about Zen.*" and I did. I told him a story from the canon of Zen tales that I knew. It was one about a Samurai swordsman who confronts a tailor for what he considered to be a breech of honor. In the story, the Samurai is defeated by the tailor's poise and commitment to die. Roye just laughed again, although this time he did not laugh quite as hardily, or lift his head that I could tell. Instead, what he did was to ask me what would have happened if the tailor went to strike the Samurai. I said I did not know. Roye then began to tell me that what would have happened is that the Samurai would not have killed the tailor, but would simply have cut his sword arm clean off. This would also have been the arm the tailor used to make a living, thereby denying the tailor the possibility of winning that day, and after the fact earning his living with his craft as he had been doing.

The story he was telling me continued with something about the tailor having to relearn everything ... how to feed himself, put on his clothing, ultimately make a living ... and so on. As he was speaking I found myself unusually tired, literally fighting to keep my eyes open. He suggested that we move to the front of the room and that I should sit on the stool next to him ... a spot of honor I thought. We did and the room full of people adjusted around us again, this time in front of us. As people settled down Roye began speaking to me again, I recognized that he was picking up on the story he had been telling, but I could not connect the pieces ... I lost the thread of where it was going completely.

It was probably then that Roye told me it would be okay to "*close your eyes*" and "*listen on the inside*" ... he told me that I could stay there, "*on the inside,*" for as long as I liked or needed to ... and to "*only come back out*" when I was done. I did not know what he meant by all that, but it made perfect sense then and there, so I just followed his instructions and kept my eyes closed. I remember hearing words on the outside, and voices other than Roye's. Every once in a while I would want to find out what was going on in the room and join them, but as my eyes would begin to flutter open Roye would suggest I just stay inside for a bit longer, "*until your done, and you've found out why you're here.*"

The whole experience of being in the Hypnotorium and meeting Roye for the first time was mesmerizing to say the least. **I had found my magician.**

Phrasing and P2hrasing

Roye had a way about him, which drew people towards him. This was somewhat remarkable. As I have described him, Roye was not a small man, he was not as young and handsome as he had once been. When I met him Roye could look downright frightening. When he was not in a mood to be trifled with Roye could turn on a kind of repulsive power that came across in his total demeanor; from his posture to the subtlest aspect of his facial expression it was clear that he was to be left alone. When he intended to send them, it was clear to anyone wise enough to pick up the signals being sent that the best choice was to back down and leave while it was still possible to do so intact.

I do not want to send any wrong messages here, I never actually saw Roye behave in a way where I questioned his judgement or behavior towards anyone. He never became physical, or even threatened to become so. His "trick" was that he could "look" that way without actually having to resort to taking any action at all. It was very effective for a couple of reasons, 1) he knew exactly how to send the message with intention (without having to be angry or annoyed to do so), and 2) I am damn sure he was perfectly capable of escalating to physical action if he needed or wanted, to do so ... and that is what came through. Let us agree to call Roye's demeanor in this regard "Interactional Aikido" - i.e.: the ability to disarm an opponent without lifting a finger and redirecting them away from confrontation before the confrontation can begin - a downright handy skill to have by the way.

Now when you take all that into account you might better understand how I say it was somewhat remarkable that Roye was typically able to draw people to him. For the most part he was perceived as a wise, elder figure ... someone who you wanted on your side and whom you believed. Even before the evidence was present you felt he could and would be there for you. I would argue that it had something to do with the eternal twinkle in his eyes, and the accompanying sparkle he could put into his voice. Maybe it was mostly his voice, that was always in

CHAPTER THREE

perfect poetic synchrony with his movements, down to the most minute and precise twitch.

Roye had one of those voices that was deep and resonant, without sounding all false radio disc-jockey like. It was truly pleasant to listen to Roye speak, from his melodious, gentle and cultured South African accent to the way he used the full range of tone, pitch and volume as he wove his stories. While he was speaking he would naturally (or seemingly so) fall into a relaxed posture, and every movement would emphasize the point he was making. If he was talking about something soft and quiet happening or a scene in which the actors were frozen he would emphasize it in the utter stillness of his own body, appearing at times not to even breathe. If he were talking about some action that was going on he would be in motion himself, his expressions, gestures and movement relating to the words spoken … including jumping up out of his chair dramatically, and sometimes terrifyingly so, to demonstrate physically what he was speaking about when he felt the impulse to do so. Of course in most cases it was subtler and somewhere between these two extremes, but in every case the effect was the same … it was mesmerizing. Roye was truly a magical and mesmerizing storyteller.

Some behavioral experts, including animal behaviorists and dog trainers, use a technical term that comes from interactional studies to describe how Roye communicated non-verbally, 'physical phrasing'. Most people are familiar with the idea of phrasing in language, i.e.: the way words are chosen to express an idea or thought, or to create a sensation or experience for the listener or reader. The term 'physical phrasing' is similar in that it refers to the way an idea or thought is expressed, or a sensation or experience is created, by virtue of the non-verbal, dynamic physical aspect of communication. These non-verbal components include posture, gesture, expression and overall movement. Physical phrasing (I'll use the term P2hrasing from now on) also carefully tracks the interactional response during communication as a critical component of communication.

I learned years before that when you are working with dogs P2hrasing is a far more critical consideration, because there is no communication without it. You simply cannot communicate with a dog using verbal spoken language alone based on the words you choose. You cannot communicate with dogs using flash cards or by randomly projecting words on a screen and expect significant, consistent responses from them ... at least not in the way you might expect to with humans. In addition, despite all the time I spent around them, I never heard of a dog moved by the most breathtaking manifesto.

You must develop excellent P2hrasing if you intend to communicate with dogs successfully (or any other species for that matter, including humans). In my experience even when they do seem to understand what you are talking to them about dogs will always override what you say and respond to what you do. You have to learn to notice for and respond to their non-verbal communication, and use that as a bridge to convey the message you intend and provoke the response you desire.

An aspect of P2hrasing in the human species is that when two people are interacting they are always subtly in motion relative to one another. They move towards and away from one another, prompted by what is happening between them. There are "response movements" designed to communicate agreement or disagreement. There are "initiatory movements" intended as invitations or rejections. There are hundreds, or thousands, of movements that could be catalogued, all of them critical to the way the communication is perceived, received and responded to during communication acts. However, this is not to imply that these movements have a fixed lexicon like words in a dictionary with absolute, standard meanings attached to them. The meaning of movement varies by context, including the culture in which they occur and the individuals participating in the dance of communication at the time.

Roye's P2hrasing was remarkably acute. He was able to synchronize his movements with the movements of another person until he could generate gross response with the subtlest change in his own behavior. In the world of NLP this is an aspect of communication that comes under the general rubric of "rapport" - referring to communicating in a way that takes into account the body-based, or somatic, communication between communicators, as well as the way you use the verbal, or semantic, component. In NLP, practitioners study what they call matching and mirroring, as well as pacing and leading. Matching refers to copying the posture, gestures and movements of another person as they do them, e.g.: right leg crossed over left leg, arms crossed on chest, head titled slightly to the left. Mirroring is the act of doing the same things to the opposite side, so that from the point of view of someone who you are face to face with in communication you are presenting a mirror image, e.g.: as per the the sequence of movement delineated above; left leg crossed over right, arms crossed on chest, head tilted slightly to the right.

In NLP terminology pacing means to follow the other person's behavioral cues, i.e.: doing what they do slightly after they do it. Leading means initiating a behavior yourself once you are in rapport so that the other person follows you and mimics your physical actions, or follows your verbal lead. When you are operating to build rapport, in the way NLP frames and refers to it, you use verbal and non-verbal communication to pace and lead, as well as matching and mirroring. Done well, using the technology of NLP, matching, mirroring, pacing and leading, both non-verbally and verbally, quickly leads to deep rapport in your communication

Psychic Rapport, Psychopaths & Wholeform Learning

I had learned to successfully build rapport using the standard NLP techniques before I met Roye and began re-learning them with him. The way I learned to do rapport in the Hypnotorium with Roye was Roye's way, which was a bit non-standard by virtue of both its precision and subtlety.

The standard way of building rapport in the NLP model is to begin pacing someone physically by matching or mirroring their posture, gestures and movements. Doing this too overtly will draw attention to you and cause you to appear to be mimicking them. If someone perceives you to be mimicking them they are likely to either a) think you are making fun of them, or b) that you're a strange character ... and neither would be particularly conducive to creating rapport. As Roye presented it building rapport was an art form, and it always began with "conversationalizing" (as I already pointed to when I described my strategy for selling).

Specifically, conversationalizing is the art of using natural conversation to build deep rapport. Roye would begin by introducing some innocuous topic, e.g.: the weather, a comment on something about the person he was speaking with, a memory that had just come to him ... or one of his favorite topics, speaking about what was current in the news.

He would just as frequently tell a story about a book he had read or movie he had seen, the topic did not matter, as long as it seemed to flow naturally within the conversation. As he spoke, Roye would engage the person he was speaking with by casually asking them questions ... getting confirmation, getting them to express an opinion of their own, or getting them to introduce a comment of their own ... even if that meant their leading the conversation elsewhere.

In conversationalizing, unlike the way I have typically seen rapport taught in most NLP training programs, the beginning point for Roye was leading not pacing. Roye would demonstrate this in the way I have described it above, introducing a topic of interest to catch the attention and begin a conversation ... most often by using an intriguing observational statement or a question. Using Roye's conversationalizing methodology to build rapport, after engaging an audience of one or many via leading, you begin pacing them verbally as they respond, e.g.: using their language and communication patterns. As the conversation unfolds you begin to deepen the state of rapport you have begun building by using very subtle and precise physical matching and mirroring, even to the point of barely shadowing the physical movements that are occurring. In this way you access the pre-conscious effect that is possible when you work outside of and beyond the threshold of ordinary conscious awareness. At some point the audience enters into a state of rapport, producing a kind of collective "shared mind" as an effect. On occasion Roye would refer to this effect as "psychic rapport" when it would produce what felt like an actual melding of minds. When what Roye called psychic rapport becomes present it seems possible to know what someone is, or would be, thinking at the same time they think it ... before it is explicitly communicated in ordinary terms.

The effect of even ordinary rapport can be magical. When it is observed it looks as though the participants are performing a choreographed routine together, one person following the other's movements in a minutely time-delayed manner. When two or more people are in deep, psychic rapport it will seem as though they are communicating telepathically, finishing one another's thoughts, spontaneously expressing one another's ideas, and even coming to conclusions with one another without any overt communication at all.

A familiar example of what could be called "psychic rapport" to many adults would be when a conclusion about engaging in consensual sex has been reached non-verbally. At some point in conversation, or during the flirtation, something shifts and it is implicitly understood by both people who are in the communication that a threshold has been crossed, and an agreement has been reached. This is a very primal experience and points to the instinctual nature of what Roye meant by psychic rapport, or what others might call deep rapport.

There are many aspects to what is happening below the surface in communication. One aspect that begins to explain why building rapport using techniques like matching and mirroring works so well might be found in human 'mirror neurons' - a specific kind of neural cell designed to pick up and "mirror" observed behavior. We see this occurring naturally in infants in their smile response. This response creates the illusion of pleasure in the infant when an adult smiles at them, although there is no real reason to believe that the infant is experiencing pleasure initially now that we know more about how mirror neurons work. However, the infant's smile response reinforces the adult connection with the infant. Typically the adult then continues the pleasant interaction reinforcing the infant's behavior and response, as well as their own. It would be reasonable to assume that after some number of iterations of this the response is welded into the infant's system, and does indeed reflect pleasure beyond mere mirroring of the adult's smile.

Mirror neurons also function as a learning adaptation. Neuroscientists that have studied mirror neuron response have found that when we watch others performing behaviorally we generate micro-muscular movements that are similar, and in some cases identical, to what we are perceiving. Literally we see others move and our bodies begin to move at the micro-muscular level in the same way. This does at least two intensely powerful things for us, 1) it allows us to experience emotional empathy because our emotions are directly related to our body responses and movement, especially at the micro-muscular level, and 2) it allows us to learn by watching others perform without having to learn in a step-by-step manner what they are able to do ... we can pre-consciously map their movements in our neuro-muscular system.

By exposure and observation we are able to use a unique approach to learning that Roye called "whole-form learning" ... literally absorbing behavioral distinctions. When we are engaged in whole-form learning, and we observe a model perform something behaviorally, we experience what they are doing at the micro-muscular level, possibly via our mirror neuron response potential, including the emotional tenor of the experience. Then as learners we then begin to replicate the performance with it pre-initiated and installed at an implicit behavioral level*.

Chapter Notes - Psychic Rapport, Psychopaths & Wholeform Learning:

*We will begin modeling and copying the behavioral performance of a "model" pre-consciously whether or not that model's behavioral performance is "perfect" or not, i.e.: we will replicate perfect and imperfect behavior at a micro-muscular level equally, and this begins to inform our experience and expectation about our own behavioral performance.

The experience of modeling in this way is also known as "deep trance identification, i.e.: DTI. When you DTI with a model intentionally - as when you set out to learn from/with them, or unintentionally - as when you watch a performer such as an athlete or dancer possibly, there is a quality to the performance that creates a kind of emotional response to it within you. The quality of the performance imprints on you in an aesthetic way, i.e.: you experience it sensorially.

High quality performances create a pleasant and desirable aesthetic experience, while poor performance creates an unpleasant experience ... in other words you feel good when you experience a high quality performance and you feel bad when you experience a poor quality performance, literally. The sensorial experience is unavoidable it seems, and highly enhanced when deep trance identifying with a model.

If your aim is learning to perform something exquisitely via DTI and behavioral modeling selecting an expert or master model to learn from is the key. When the primary learning strategy is modeling, the ability of the model to demonstrate the performance you intend to replicate is at least as significant as their ability to teach what they know.

Picking a great model/teacher becomes especially important when you consider that the experience of learning is imprinted at a micro-muscular level, creating a sensation of physical attraction or repulsion that becomes associated with the behavior being learned ... and, unfortunately, sometimes with the model who is performing it as well.

However, when a model/teacher/mentor can both masterfully demonstrate a behavioral performance and teach what they do well they are a truly precious commodity to come by - in my experience such individuals are worth more, and are rarer to find than the "prima materia" of an alchemist.

CHAPTER THREE

An Extreme Example:
Mirror Neurons and the Natural Use and Limits of P2hrasing

We live in "in-human" times with regard to our ability to access and employ some of our most precious biological gifts, earned over the many hundreds of millennia of human evolution. Most people living today in affluent, first-world, industrialized environments with access to unprecedented creature comforts and security, i.e.: most or all of the people ever likely to read this, are totally ignorant and delusional when it comes to using human P2hrasing and its effect in their lives.

We have been raised to assume that altruism and empathy are to be expected from others, and we have learned to interact and respond as though they will always be present. We assume "good intention" and live with an expectation that we are entitled to be treated well and kindly by others. This is simply not the ordinary biological standard for humans engaging outside of kinship or tribal bonds.

By example, a well known animal behavior in some animal species is that males - especially non-biologically related males, and in some instances directly biologically related males including the father, can pose a threat to young infants including perpetrating an act of infanticide. This kind of behavior is often recorded in primate species, and present in homo sapiens, i.e.: ordinary modern humans. Seldom does the average person even consider that it is "normal" for an adult human male to experience thoughts of infanticide, but it is perfectly normal at an evolutionary, biological level to think that this could, or even would, be the case*.

We have built-in biological mechanisms that tend to limit the danger we potentially present to one another that fall under the general rubric of human P2hrasing. The smile response of infants seems to defuse the innate impulse to violence that some adult males display toward infant children. This is one example of the positive effect of naturally occurring P2hrasing in communication. This is compounded by familiarity in vocal tonality and smell that tend to create emotional bonding between adult males and their offspring or kin.

During display behavior in the sympathetic portion of the ANS mirror neurons may serve a survival function in the species throughout the lifespan as well. The smile response may also apply when we are attempting to diffuse escalation to violence as adults with other adults, or to draw others into our circle of influence. When we smile, or laugh, others often respond in kind ... essentially their mirror neurons kick-in and take over at a pre-conscious, micro-muscular reflex level of response. A theoretical consideration is that our mirror neurons may allow us to know something of the mind of others, i.e.: to guess at what they may be experiencing by running an echo of their externally expressed behaviors as micro-muscular responses in our own neurological system.

When this occurs the thinking of the other person follows the line of the response orchestrated by their mirror neurons physically, i.e.: when we are smiling or laughing we assume we are comfortable, safe and feel good. When we have this response towards another person, unless other factors overrule the innate response, we begin to feel connected to them ... and comfortable, safe and good with them.

As a survival mechanism mirror neuron action, such as the smile response, is a brilliant social adaptation when it is present in small, biologically contained and connected tribal groups. When this kind of mechanism is present (and it is) in large, messy, dense societies it allows for human predators to deploy it to their advantage.

The most current thinking suggests that those most likely employ deceptive behavior for malicious ends are those who are least compelled psychologically not to do so. According to current psychological research most people have a natural inhibition to behaving in an evil, malicious way that goes counter to the expression of ordinary altruism and/or empathy, and the emotions associated with acting in this way. Some of the same social psychologists who study the responses of ordinary altruism and empathy have also studied and suggested that sociopaths do not have the typical ability to experience altruism, empathy or the emotional responses that limit malicious behavior in most people.

Sociopaths, due to their lack of inhibition in acting maliciously towards others for their own ends, are able to assume behaviors that indicate friendliness, connection or caring when their intentions are diametrically opposed without the telltale indicators the would expose them. The intentions of sociopaths can range from simple malingering to homicidal malfeasance. They may only want to get by with doing little or nothing, and having someone provide for them in some material, sexual, intellectual or social manner.

Some sociopaths prey on others with greater deliberation, such as those engaged in the "con game" - grifters, swindlers, embezzlers and larcenists. Sociopaths can also be responsible for the most reprehensible criminal acts, horrors and atrocities known, from serial rape and/or murder to genocide. One expert** also suggests that many powerful individuals in both business and politics display classic sociopath behaviors and express themselves in those spheres in ways that are more socially acceptable, despite being sociopathic.

Because they lack the ordinary inhibitions of altruism, empathy and emotional response the behavioral performances of sociopaths carry little to none of the markers of deception that would be present in the interactional behavior of a non-sociopathic individual. Because they have no markers of deception, sociopaths can get past the natural instinctive and intuitive defenses humans have built in over eons of evolution in reading the emotional response and mental state of others, even when they harbor the most evil and malicious intentions.

Should you ever be confronted with the kind of extreme evil or malicious behavior that only a sociopath would be capable of, knowing explicitly how human P2hrasing works in communication helps to limit the affect it will have on you. When you are not automatically and completely taken in by their masterful use of emotional acting and their behavioral performances intended to influence and disarm you via your own naturally occurring altruistic, empathic and emotional responses, you remain capable of making higher quality decisions and choices. In a potentially dangerous or deadly situation with a sociopath your knowledge of human P2hrasing and its effect may be the first and only defense available to you. Literally, in this type of situation not becoming a victim in the first place may be your only salvation.

*Sarah Hardy, a Harvard primatologist who has studied many species of primates in their forest habitats, noted that adult male infanticide has been reported for all the major groups of higher primates: monkeys, the great apes and man. NY Times: INFANTICIDE: ANIMAL BEHAVIOR SCRUTINIZED FOR CLUES TO HUMANS, Bayard Webster, Published: August 17, 1982 (http://tiny.cc/thutyw)

**Robert D. Hare, Ph.D., creator of the Hare Psychopathy Checklist, and the author of "*Without Conscience: The Disturbing World of the Psychopaths Among Us*" (1999) and "*Snakes in Suits: When Psychopaths Go to Work*" (2006)

Chapter Four:
The Chalice and the Crucible

"Deep in the human unconscious is a pervasive need for a logical universe that makes sense.

But the real universe is always one step beyond logic."

- Frank Herbert
Dune

CHAPTER FOUR

Swallowing the Canary Whole

"The chalice that contains the magic elixir for elite human performance is generally labeled learning ... however in my opinion it would be more accurately labeled 'whole-form' learning."
- Joseph Riggio, Ph.D.

My experience learning from, and working with, Roye led me to believe that he was most interested in doing transformational work. He wanted to lead his clients beyond the limitations they were experiencing, not incrementally, in a step-by-step fashion, but in a single whole-form movement where the limitations they had been experiencing simply did not - and could not - exist. To this end Roye's default process of working with clients, individually and in groups, relied on his use of whole-form learning. I spent many years observing and absorbing whole-form learning before I even realized that was what I was experiencing.

**Roye's approach to creating transformation using whole-form learning was always designed to ...
"Go to where the problem is not!"**

Whole-form learning ("W-learning" from this point forward) is both remarkably common and extremely rare. That may seem like a paradox, but it is not. As human beings we learn most things naturally through W-learning, e.g.: most or all of the things psychologists refer to as "developmental" learning, the process of maturing and the knowledge and skills we incorporate by virtue of the maturation process. Think of all the things you've learned to do, without ever formally learning them. We learn to read the signals of emotion before anyone explicitly teaches them to us. Most adults have an 'instinct' or 'intuition' that lets them know when someone is sad or glad, angry or anxious, in pain or perky ... weak and sickly or robust and healthy.

When we say things, using an idiom like, "**You look like you've swallowed a canary.**" ... wink, wink, we are commenting based on two things, 1) an instinctual understanding of how to read emotion signals and 2) a learned use of metaphor. We use a metaphor about what would make a cat happy and guilty at the same time, where the cat represents the person we are commenting about of course.

Metaphor works by allowing us to substitute one thing for another that stands in for the thing we are referring to indirectly. An unspecified reference to a cat substitutes for the person being referred to in the example above, and relies on an intuitive understanding of the idiom to make any sense. Metaphors allow us to communicate more than what our words alone say ... and we learn how to make the connections that metaphor points to without any formal education required to teach us how to do so via W-learning.

Along the same lines we also learn in whole-form seemingly simpler things that are in fact remarkably complex. We learn things like judging where objects are in space relative to us ... even when they are in motion ... "**CATCH!**" We learn naturally to unravel the mystery that just because an object disappears for a moment when it moves behind another object that blocks it from our view that it is not gone ... "**PEEK-A-BOO!**" We learn other commonplace complex things as well, that most people would never consider as "learning," e.g.: how to control our bladders and bowels ... "**DO YOU HAVE TO GO?**"

As we continue to mature we also continue learning remarkably complex things. Sometimes what we are learning seems complex to us as we are learning it, and sometimes not. An example of a complex learning task would be, "**Does that boy or girl like me?**", and how to tell when they do, before they say so. All of the learning in the examples above and more like them occur within W-learning contexts, and this learning is incredibly important to becoming a high functioning adult in the world we live in together.

Two supreme examples of W-learning that naturally occur for humans, are walking and talking. Both of these are remarkable behavioral performances that a vast majority of humans master without any "formal" learning in terms of the way learning is ordinarily considered. A strong argument has been made by neuroscientists that mirror neurons play a major role in the iterative, recursive loops regarding behavioral modeling and performance in the learning process, leading up to learning complex behavioral tasks like becoming masterful "walkers" and "talkers." Despite the fact that almost all people with the facility to do so learn to walk and talk, both are feats of extraordinary complexity. The same W-learning process we used to become "walkers" and "talkers" can be used in learning virtually anything we desire. I would make the argument that our mirror neurons are uniquely designed to allow for W-learning, and that nature intended for us to learn our most important life lessons via W-learning.

W-learning is always a behavioral process. As I see it, the act of learning is behavioral, the process of inputting what we learn is behavioral, and the subsequent outputting of learning is also behavioral. Things like learning to walk and talk have clear behavioral components, i.e.: the actions of walking and talking. However, under the umbrella of 'behavior' I also include all acts of cognition, like learning to do arithmetic or complex mathematics. Contrary to popular thought, "thinking" is always somatic and involves the use of our bodies. Thinking is somatically organized and referenced. By default, humans are embodied thinkers and thinking is a behavior just like walking and talking.

At some point in their lives many people experience difficulty in learning, in one way or another. Some people learn how to achieve academically with natural ease, others find the same things difficult. There are people with remarkable athletic facility who learn how to use their bodies in ways that would be impossible for others. The key to successful learning is aligning the learning process with what is being learned and the learner who is learning.

Most natural human performance, like walking and talking, throwing and catching objects, reading emotion and intention in others … is best approached via W-learning. Some things, like academic conceptual or abstract topics may be best approached using traditional, formal learning organized more linearly, i.e.: in a step-by-step fashion. Examples of topics that may be best approached using this kind of learning are primarily sequential and rule based like arithmetic … although some forms of advanced mathematics, like calculus or topology, may still be best approached using W-learning, because as much anything else they require a "feel" for the topic as well as an intellectual understanding.

Learning becomes difficult or impossible when the learning style is not well matched to what is being learned and the learner. People are constitutionally organized to learn certain kinds of things more easily than others for many different reasons. One of the things that makes a great teacher great is their ability to recognize the natural learning patterns that someone uses and align the way they teach to the way individuals learn, rather than using a "one size fits all" approach.

When a learner fails to learn the first thing to address is the learning and teaching style being used, NOT the motivation or the ability of the learner. The motivation and the ability of the teacher is often far more important to what is learned, or not, than the motivation and ability of the learner. There are endless examples I could point to, but one that stands out is the example of Helen Keller and Anne Sullivan who exceeded every expectation that could have been applied to their situation at the time. What Anne Sullivan did for Helen Keller was to include the entirety of her in an embodied W-learning process ... body, mind and soul.

Although some would argue that not all learning is W-learning, it would be much harder to argue that all learning is not ultimately embodied. Embodiment in human learning refers to the idea that we are beings with bodies and those bodies are always in some situated context. Both of these things, your body and the situated context are part of the process of thinking and learning. One aspect of embodiment is that as you experience mental activity of any kind simultaneous responses occur in your body that we can refer to as feelings. Your feelings then become part of the feedback loop that shapes your mental process, i.e.: thinking ... and the loop continues iteratively and recursively as you continue to respond physically to what you are thinking.

W-learning assumes and accepts that whatever you are feeling, i.e.: the responses in your body - including those that are the basis of emotion, becomes the ground of thinking. How you feel shapes how you think regardless of what you are responding to internally and/or externally. The exchange that occurs between what you are feeling, what you are thinking and the environment or context you find yourself contained within, including the data that is present and emergent, form the basis of W-learning.

Responding to the totality of your experience behaviorally allows you to create outcomes that are specifically suited to the situated context.

CHAPTER FOUR

When your experience of the environment takes into account the totality that is present your behaviors will be better shaped and suited to create the outcomes you intend. An advantage of W-learning is that it allows you to update and continuously learn in real time as the situation changes. Based on W-learning your responses keep pace regardless of how the circumstance or situation changes, and you are able to move towards the outcome you intend.

The process of W-learning seems to most often operate within a context defined by a few specific common restraints:

A) We must have the innate facility to learn what we are attempting to accomplish behaviorally, e.g.: to see stereo optically we must have two eyes.

B) Whole-form learning is greatly enhanced if we have a suitable model we can learn from, e.g.: when we can observe a model performing behaviorally we can imprint the behavior in our neuro-somatic system, as well as in our neuro-cognitive system, before we know how to consciously or deliberately replicate it ourselves.

C) Our willingness to work at refining our behavior to reach the level of skillfulness we intend will largely determine the level of proficiency we attain.

Transferring W-learning from an implicit to explicit level requires repetition and refinement. We need to continue the learning process until our entire neurological system has incorporated it at a fine enough level to control our sensory system, emotive response and the active functional somatic and cognitive processes required to replicate the learned performance at the desired level of skillfulness. As learning is occurring these processes are running simultaneously. W-learning happens as part of an innate, cybernetic system ... where all things are iteratively and recursively informed by and informing one another as the system updates and makes the necessary adjustments overall.

The learning process seems to be radically enhanced via observation by a skilled observer who is able and willing to assist the learner in making the required refinements to achieve the desired behavioral outcome. In a W-learning context a modeler who takes on the role of "coach," "teacher," "trainer" or "mentor" can greatly enhance this process by knowing what to emphasize in their own performance, and in the sequencing of what they model and how they model it for the learner. When specific sensory experiences, emotions and functional responses are skillfully provoked they create feedback loops that assist the learner in attaining behavioral performances at the desired level of skillfulness and proficiency.

In W-learning the modeler doesn't necessarily have to be able to create the performance that the learner is aiming for themselves. For instance a masterful coach may know how to elicit and provoke elite performance from players on a team, in the same way that a gifted conductor can draw out and shape the performance of an orchestra … without necessarily possessing the skillfulness of the performers for whom they are building the model of performance. They can do this because the "model" can be and is shaped in the space the coach/conductor and the performers occupy and share. To do this however they must know how their own behaviors affect the performances of others, how to shape those performances and possess the requisite behavioral flexibility, resilience and skillfulness to create the desired outcome with and for others.

Roye was uniquely skillful in his ability to model behavior that moved me forward towards achieving my desired outcomes, and to simultaneously act as a professional observer assisting me in refining my behaviors to my intended level of skillfulness. He was a superb model who could and easily did elicit and provoke powerful responses from me as necessary, often holding and operating in more than one position at a time. His absolute insistence on maintaining a W-learning context made the approach he took particularly powerful.

People benefit in learning in the way that nature intended us to learn, using all of our innate facilities to survive, prosper and thrive. The years I spent apprenticing at the knee of the master unconsciously molded me into a master in the design and use of W-learning as well. Now I reside in an atmosphere where W-learning as natural to my experience as the air around me is rich in the oxygen I depend upon to breathe. This is in part the legacy of my living in the rarified, mediated space of W-learning around Roye for more than a decade.

After more than two decades of working with clients using W-learning I know there is no way to replicate that transformational experience of spending time with a skillful coach, teacher, trainer or mentor who works in this way as the basis of the approach they take with coachees/students/clients. I have made W-learning the default process I use to coach, teach, train and mentor everyone who wants to learn with me. It is also the reason so few "make it" my way … they are unwilling or unable to give up their expectation of "how learning is supposed to happen."

Most folks suckled on traditional, formal learning refuse to reside within the W-learning structure of the Hero's Journey long enough to receive the boon, the gift, the elixir, the totem or whatever their particular personal reward is … that Joseph Campbell tells us awaits the hero at the end of their Adventure. Almost everyone I meet wants the Luke Skywalker experience as they watch him live his Adventure through to the end … but, so few are willing to stay the course. All Roye ever asked was simply …

"Keep your sole in the room, and while you are here, let your soul guide you."

Ontologically Speaking …

The most critical distinction that I learned in all my years with Roye was that everything rests on and begins from a consideration of Being … 'Who' … not What, When, Where, How or Why. "Who are you?" or "Who am I?" was the question that drove everything Roye did, and I learned from him, even when the question was silent.

Part of the crazy-making process of studying with Roye was the subtlety of the shift from the question asked to the question being answered. Roye would almost always start with the question, **"What do you want?"** when he began working with someone. I cannot tell you how many times I was asked the question, **"What do you want?"** and how many times in the Hypnotorium I answered it … or the number of times my request remained unanswered …

In the first months of learning from Roye I took the question literally … "What do you want?" … so I might answer, "I want to know how to use anchoring (a classic NLP technique)?" … and he would say,

"Fine.", then move on to the next person, asking them the same question ... and leaving me sitting, waiting for an answer that would never come. Finally Roye would get to someone and ask them the question and they would say something ridiculous like, "I want to be free." or better yet "I want the sun." ... and he would fawn over them, or so it seemed.

So that's the way it would go in the Hypnotorium, week after week. I would ask for something reasonable and Roye would leave me wanting for a response unfulfilled. Then someone would ask for something ridiculous, e.g.: "I want the sun" and he would fixate on them for two hours, doing what I later learned he called "private work" with them, publicly in the group. Afterwards, he would turn to the rest of us, point to an easel with a large pad on it where he had written out a classic NLP exercise, and tell us to "Go and do the exercise." ... which I and everyone else in the room understood to mean use the exercise written out on the pad as the basis to replicate what he had just done in front of us. He could have just as well asked us to hold our breath for twenty minutes, or hold out our hand and conjure a pineapple out of the thin air we were not supposed to be breathing.

Unseen by me for months, Roye was using the question, "What do you want?" more literally than I could possible have understood at the time ... meaning he really did want to get to what each person desired and expected to get by being in the room with him. What I did was listen to the answer and assume that whatever was being asked for was to be linked to a set of steps to be taken to accomplish the outcome requested ... like I had learned to expect in the previous sixteen or so years of schooling I had attended. The crazy-making came from never hearing an answer, that made any sense to me for months, to the question that was being asked or to the response given. However, what Roye "listened" for was something else entirely, something utterly unknowable to me then.

Roye would never give anyone a series of steps to take about anything, except for what he'd written out about how to run an exercise we were doing as part of the training program. Instead, he would begin talking about something entirely off topic, usually beginning by telling a story from his own life, or maybe from something he had read, or a plot from a movie he had seen ... "conversationalizing" with the group at large. I thought either he was not listening to the responses he got, did not care what the answers were ... or maybe he was hard of hearing, because he clearly did not hear what I heard based on the responses he gave ... if and when he bothered to respond. Actually, in the beginning it was often more crazy-making to get an answer from Roye, than for him to ignore the fact that I had spoken.

What I did not know at the start, was that what Roye was listening for in the answer to the question "What do you want?" was "WHO" was answering the question ... and even more exotically, "WHO" would the speaker have to be, or become, to have come up with whatever they were saying.

While listening to "WHO" someone has to be to have what it is they say they want is exotic ... it is not esoteric.

The evidence about "WHO" someone must become is readily available if you know what to listen to, and look for, when you ask the question, "What do you want?" ... because no on can answer that question without becoming "WHO" they are when they have whatever it is they say they want. Even if that way of being only appears for an instant in regard to what they want they must make the leap to who they will have to be upon having whatever it is they want. When we say, "I want ..." and complete the sentence, in that moment we project ourselves to the imaginal experience of having that desire fully satisfied. It is experiencing what it is to have what we are asking for that drives us to want it and the sense we possess of the satisfaction we will have when we get it. Maybe what we want is relief from something we perceive to be missing, or something that we want relief from that is present and painful to us, the "wanting" is the expression of that relief being realized and WHO we are when that is true of us.

Part of Roye's "magic" was his ability to catch "WHO" the person was in that imaginal instant of their complete and utter satisfaction. "WHO" here refers to how they were explicitly being in their moment of fulfillment. Roye would begin working with them from there, holding that space where being complete, whole, satisfied and fulfilled was present for them, while they could not hold it for themselves yet ... making it explicit and creating access as he offered them the hypnotic suggestion to insure it would remain available to them "on-words."

In some circles the debate between what "Being" means can go on and on and on ... ad infinitum. It is a slippery concept and topic of discussion because it will depend on what school of thought you are approaching it from, e.g.: if you come at "Being" from a spiritual or religious frame it may take you in one direction, if you come at it from a philosophical, metaphysical frame it takes you in another. With Roye I learned to understand the concept of "Being" differently, literally ... based on dynamic observation of emergent patterns in someone's responses. When we respond to anything, a question, a change of temperature in the room, a fly buzzing about our head, something we ate for lunch that was disgusting or delightful, we respond ... and we respond first and foremost somatically, physically, in and with our bodies, and we are a particular way in that moment, i.e.: we are "being" in some way.

From Roye, I learned to pay attention to my somatic experience and the somatic response I had to inform me about whatever it was that was happening in terms of what it meant to and for me. When I could do that effectively, I automatically began to notice how others around me were responding somatically, often knowing before they did themselves that they were responding at all. The somatic process is very fast compared to the ordinary cognitive process ... usually happening before a person can "think" in ordinary cognitive terms.

Long before you create representations, calculate and process what is happening around you, you are responding somatically, i.e.: physically in and with your body, to anything and everything you experience. When you are speaking with someone as you calculate what they are saying, and what their words mean ... you are responding to and processing somatically the tone of their voice, their movements and even things like their distance from you or closeness to you.

If you have been raised in a modern society, have attended school, are educated ... and typical ... you either do not know you are responding somatically, or ignore it, until after you have calculated the meaning of the words you hear when someone is speaking. Then ... again, assuming you are typical ... you will account for the way you feel by associating it with the words you heard, making them by default responsible for how you are feeling about them (the words) ... when in reality the words meant what you calculated they did in part because of how you felt when you were hearing them.

CHAPTER FOUR

Your somatic responses and feelings happen first ... before your cortical, cognitive responses, i.e.: what you notice yourself thinking

When I learned about this from Roye, and incorporated this learning into my experience as a fundamental principal guiding how I operated and acted in the world, my life changed. This learning radically altered how I experienced my relationships with others, how I made decisions about what to be doing or not, and who I knew myself to be in an ongoing way. Specifically I began to know myself in large part by how I was responding in and through my body, letting my body lead my mind for a while as I was learning about this new way of being.

RADICAL ... I KNOW!

There are five additional critical components I would point to in my years learning with Roye:

1) Roye provoked me to express the behaviors I wanted to have intentional, conscious access to on demand, before I knew I was capable of expressing those behaviors myself

2) Roye helped me to realize that more important than having access to specific behaviors was the ability to generate and maintain an attitude conducive to producing the results I intended

3) Roye taught me the first step in getting what I wanted was establishing what he called the Generalized Desired State (GDS), a positively organized overarching operating position that creates a massive sense of directionality, or pull, towards expressing the behaviors necessary to produce intended outcomes as my default operating position

4) Roye modeled the use of hypnotic communication protocols to induce learning that was out of my conscious awareness; using hypnotic learning as a powerful means available to

provoke new behaviors, initiate and install new attitudes, and to evoke and establish the GDS as my essential operating position

5) Roye exposed me to the idea that all learning and all behaviors, including cognition and speech acts, are state dependent; and that all states are fundamentally about Being, i.e.: ontological, and only secondarily about knowing or ways of knowing, i.e.: epistemological

This last point about starting with an ontological versus epistemological consideration is critical to understanding what I experienced in my learning with Roye. Epistemology addresses how we know what we know, what is true as we know it and how we know it to be true. This is the ground of all beliefs and values. Ontology on the other hand addresses the fundamental question of what is extant, or what is Being, e.g.: "Who am I?" It is the ground of all experience, including all "states." Another way of thinking about epistemology and ontology is that we must first "be" before we can "know" … so ontology must by default precede epistemology.

This question about an ontological orientation versus an epistemological orientation, or beginning from being before knowing, is significant to the transformation I was pursuing. It changes all the questions being asked, and therefore all the answers that follow. What I thought I wanted when I first approached Roye was to attain a certification as a Master Practitioner and then to become a Trainer of NLP. I thought I was there to learn and gain new skills. What quickly became evident to me as I continued working with Roye was that it was first much more important to discover who I fundamentally was, and am, at my core.

Over that first long weekend, when I met Roye in Pemberton at the Blue Dell Farm Hypnotorium, he began to provoke in me a sense of my ontological core.

It is not hard to find sources pointing to "Being" as the core of what it is to be human. The challenge with pointing to "Being" (versus

"Doing" for instance) is that it seems elusive and hard to capture. Yet despite this challenge virtually everyone I have ever met, and as well as myself, experience that we are somehow "more" than our behaviors and/or actions, or the results we produce though them. We intuit "Being" at the core of who we are as we conceive of ourselves. Many people also intuit or have faith in Being beyond themselves, e.g.: a personal "G-d" or a plethora of gods ... "Nature" with a capital "N" as Frank Lloyd Wright the famous American architect and Universalist Unitarian posited ... "Spirit" imbuing all things ... the Universe or Cosmos as a sentient entity of its own ... there are an astounding number of ways people throughout the ages have come up with explaining their encounter with Being beyond themselves.

Many people either consider themselves to have a direct connection or relationship with whatever they hold to be Being beyond themselves, e.g.: "G-d" - and that relationship can be either personal or impersonal. Others consider themselves to be part of what they hold to be a greater Being than they individually represent. Some consider themselves to be a contained, local representation of the macro Being as a micro expression of it. Still others consider themselves to be the totality of Being itself, having an experience of non-duality, i.e.: the are Being itself, and they refer to all that they experience beyond the purity of Beingness as "illusion."

Regardless of how we individually consider Being and Being Beyond Ourselves, it seems part of the innate human condition to perceive some essential ground from which all of our experience emerges and on which we have what we call experience. Maybe the simplest way to express this is,

"Regardless of all else that we may or may not know and/or believe, we accept that we ourselves exist."

Rene Descartes' famous philosophical expression: **"Cogito Ergo Sum"** ... "I think, therefore I am." expressed the idea of Being as an epistemological function, or a function of thinking. This put Being into the service of thought. Yet the premise I began to experience with Roye was a direct awareness of Being as the ground from which thought emerged.

In the Hypnotorium with Roye, in my very first three days with him, I began to have a direct perception and awareness of Being without representation or thought. I was becoming aware of myself as the ground of my thoughts ... including my beliefs and values. Everything I thought and believed to be true, or to be untrue, I began to perceive as projection of myself and not as something "out there" in the world "as is."

From my first days with Roye, Descartes' famous saying began to twist and spin for me becoming, "Ergo Sum Cogito" ... "I am, therefore I think."

By the end of my initial encounter with Roye I came to accept that all of my thinking ... my thoughts, considerations, beliefs, values ... was a function of Being, **"Who I Am."** The notion that all I thought I knew and understood manifested as an expression of **"Who I Am"** was profound and radically transformative. I left those three days possessed by the thought that I must find out who I was Being, how that was constructed and how I held it in place. I was truly on a holy quest, a sacred journey, to uncover the source of my Being.

Although over the years we would speak of these things many times, Roye never once spoke of any of this with me or the group on that first weekend when I originally met him. He never to my recollection mentioned "Being" or "Beingness." He never in that weekend spoke of "ontology" as I remember it. However, despite that fact that it was never explicitly spoken, in the entirety of what I experienced in those three days the implicit specter of Being and Beingness loomed over me.

"Who Am I?" ... this fundamental question drove me. I simply had to find out who I was at my core ... I needed to know **"Who I Am."** I knew this with the same degree of certainty that I knew I had to return to the Hypnotorium and learn from this man. I also knew that once I crossed that threshold, stepped onto that path and into that journey there would be no turning back ... and in that presumption I was correct.

Beginning to Become Myself Again

CHAPTER FOUR

What helped to drive the new compulsion I was experiencing "to find myself" were two aspects of the experience that became inseparable ...

First Roye helped me to quiet my mind, to focus on my internal awareness as the primary experience I was having, dismissing to a great extent - at least for the moment - all external stimuli. I simply stopped caring about what was going on outside of myself. With my eyes closed, sitting on a stool next to Roye in Pemberton, I shut off the external visual data stream. Although I could and did still hear the sounds in the room, Roye had instructed me to ignore them and fix my attention on my internal experience instead, and I followed his suggestion absolutely.

One effect of focusing internally was that the sounds outside of myself became muted and unintelligible to me, a kind of pink noise beyond my ability to attend to it in any meaningful way. I later learned that this sound is also what I have come to associate with the sound of silence, which is not silent at all ... in fact it can sometimes roar at me insistently.

Secondly, I was remarkably physically relaxed and balanced ... sitting poised on the stool at the front of the Hypnotorium. In short order I began to feel like I either did not have a body to support, or that it was floating in a perfectly balanced and weightless way. My senses began to relax as my body continued to relax.

I remember the strongest sensory experience that remained was the scent of Roye sitting next to me.

I have always been particularly sensitive to smell. In Roye's case it was a subtle combination of smoke and muskiness. The musk smell was not dissimilar to the smells I had encountered when I had been in the deep forest. It was akin to the primal smell of nature or life as I thought about it. I recognized the smell immediately, as it was a smell I had noticed I had myself at times when I was in a highly charged state ... when I was engaged in something particularly exciting or challenging. It was the same smell just before I was about to fight in competition, a mixture of contained fear and exhilaration ... sometimes when I was training dogs, especially when I was doing intense protection work with them, when I was in a bit of danger and needed to be at the top of my game with them ... it was also the smell of sex, the lingering scent of my body when it was sexually charged, both in the process leading up to and after a sexual encounter with a woman.

I recognized the smell behind the smokiness of Roye's cigarette as the scent of life ... pure, primal life, throbbing with fecund possibility at the edge of the unknown ... and I realized that I too began to smell that way as I sat there ... and I liked it.

Occasionally Roye would make a comment directly to me, almost in passing. He would not say my name or call out to me when he did this, yet I knew that he was speaking directly to me. It was part of the overall conversation he was having with the group, but somehow he marked out what he was saying so I would rouse a bit and notice it, and realize that it was something explicitly being said for my benefit. As these comments and suggestions built I found myself more and more distanced from the room I was in, and more and more internally focused. It was as though I were sinking into myself. After some time I was only aware of myself as a body. I could not for the life in me perceive thoughts as I normally think them. For the most part this meant I was not aware of using words, talking to myself or describing the experience I was having to myself. I did not have a sense of any other time, there was only the moment I was in ... no past, no future that I could conceive of in any meaningful way, shape or form ... only now, now, now ... in unending stream of individual, unconnected moments.

I shifted from thinking to just Being as far as my experience in the world was concerned. I was certain without any thought about it in that moment, that I was my body. I experienced myself as a primal being experiencing myself and everything else as an affect of my body, what I would now call a direct sensory experience that was somatically based and organized. Literally, what I was experiencing in and with my body was everything as far as I was concerned in that moment ... there was nothing else beyond that ... it was total and complete.

The most profound peace and calm emerged in me during that time. I was utterly relaxed and utterly ready. It was a sensation unlike any I could recall knowing, paradoxically comforting and unfamiliar. I felt like there was nothing to do ... nothing I could do and nothing I could not do, I was holding what I would have called an absolute paradox and it felt like the most natural thing in the world to me. I was hanging on the

CHAPTER FOUR

edge of readiness. I later learned how important this idea of "readiness" was to the work I was beginning to encounter and experience with Roye.

After I came out of that experience, I immediately updated my previous commitment to myself about becoming a NLP Trainer that I had made the evening I spend with Richard Bandler. I decided I would learn first how to access and remain "ready" in the way I was as I sat on that stool next to Roye. I also decided I would continue to sit next to him for as long as it took to replicate what he led me to with others.

Instinctively I knew that remaining "ready" in the way Roye had led me to experience it was the proverbial skeleton key to unlocking everything I had ever wanted. I also knew without doubt that it was the simplest, most essential and natural thing in the world to do. The experience I had sitting on that stool in the Hypnotorium with Roye allowed me to dismiss all the unfulfilled desires I had ever held before that experience. What I wanted became the most obvious and simplest thing imaginable, I want "THIS" ... the experience I had on that stool ... and I wanted it without cessation or exception. There was nothing I needed to fix first, or have, or become, before I could have "THIS" ... the readiness I now knew was possible for me in that instant. I experienced the crucible of profound transformation, and once I had experienced it there was no way back to who I had been ... I had already become someone else.

I also had an inkling that this was what I had always been trying to reach when I thought about "Being." I was a student of the writing of the Zen masters and the Taoists. I had read thousands of pages of philosophy by then too, and I was still a good Catholic boy deep down, although I had long since stopped formally practicing according to the Church. For years I had been seeking the experience of pure Being without know it or calling it that. One of my favorite authors, Carlos Castaneda wrote about it as "Stopping the World." Finally I had it ... this was the resolution of ontological longing. Instead of desperately doing anything and everything in the search to "find myself" and "know who I am" I had it completely and fully for those precious moments. I bought in hook, line and sinker.

What I did not know was how Roye had done what he did with me. I chalked it up at the time to his magnificent skills as a NLP Master Trainer and Master Hypnotist, but it was much more than that. There are NLP Trainers and Master Trainers I met over the years who could not begin to do what Roye did with me. I have met remarkable hypnotists who do amazing work with clients, and they too could not begin to replicate the effect of the first five minutes I had in the Hypnotorium.

After years experiencing innumerable hours under Roye's guidance, watching him work with other people for thousands of hours, having him correct and guide my actions and working with thousands of people myself, I finally began to unravel the mystery of what made what he did with me so powerful. It was a perfect demonstration of W-learning, Roye was the vehicle for what he was teaching me. There was no separation in any way or at any level in what I was experiencing, I was experiencing what I was learning, and learning what I was experiencing …

Chapter Five:
The Game Called, "Life"

"...when you have eliminated all which is impossible, then whatever remains, however improbable, must be the truth."
- Sherlock Holmes

- Arthur Conan Doyle
The Blanched Soldier

CHAPTER FIVE

Illusions and Delusions

Despite how powerfully W-learning naturally works we seldom encounter it in formal education, i.e.: in schools. Instead of W-learning, from the time we are young children, say between the ages of five or six, we are educated in a fragmented, distorted way. In school we are introduced to the idea of "subjects," in a way that causes ideas, concepts and entire fields of study to appear separate from one another. Because our learning experience separates things in the way it does, it causes us to think of things as separate. Experiencing separation between things becomes true for us even when they are contained in and are part of a larger system. Even when things are clearly not separate when considered from a whole-form point of view, because of bad learning, we often experience them as separate.

This feeds into another distortion, **the illusion of cause and effect**, which always seems to makes perfect sense after the fact... but does not always make sense before the fact.

[**Author's Note:** *If "cause and effect" thinking worked as well as we are taught it does, our decision-making would be much better informed, and the results we produce based on our assumptions would be much closer to our expectations than is often the case.*]

Along with the distortions of separation, and cause and effect thinking, we are often taught in a linear, sequential way, e.g.: step-by-step; with the steps of an activity presented as though they stand apart, conceptually separated, just like subject matter. Because of the context, and the way we are taught, from a young age, our conception of what learning is or should be takes form beyond the reach of our conscious awareness. Very quickly we begin to accept that things, virtually all things, are best organized and learned, in a step-by-step manner. As a result of how we are taught we come to expect information, and almost everything else in our lives, to be presented to us in that way, with debilitating implications.

1) Learning that information is best organized and learned in a step-by-step fashion causes us to stop the learning process until we have mastered the step we are on; when we do not or cannot master the learning step we are on we become stuck in the learning process ... sometimes permanently.

E.g.: When this happens to a child in school it can be tragic for them and their experience as a student, unless it gets remedied quickly they start to fail in the subject matter completely.

2) The world seldom presents information to us in a step-by-step, take your time and do one thing after another, manner ... think about avoiding a car that has run a red light when you expected it to stop.

E.g.: If you took your time to work out in a step-by-step manner what was happening, and what you needed to do, in many situations you would not survive for long in this world - and it would have been worse for our hunter/gatherer ancestors, our species never would have made it.

3) In human relations the expectation that things will and do occur logically, step-by-step, with one event logically following another ... i.e.: linear, sequential, cause and effect thinking ... creates havoc in relationships.

E.g.: From intimate romantic relationships that fail, to disruptions and the despair that follows them in families, to the persistent insanity of modern business beginning in the boardroom ... we see endless examples of how linear, sequential, cause and effect thinking fails us.

4) As we experience change - especially chaotic change - working out what is happening as it is happening, and figuring out how to respond using linear, sequential, cause and effect thinking simply does not serve us.

CHAPTER FIVE

E.g.: Seldom if ever can this kind of thinking keep up with the speed at which life happens, and it virtually never produces responses with enough flexibility, resiliency and creativity to allow us to consistently respond in a way that produces the outcomes we expect and desire.

(**Author's Note:** *For simplicities sake I will replace the entire phrase "linear, sequential, cause and effect" with just the words "cause and effect" from this point forward.*)

The Universe we live in is not designed in a fragmented cause and effect fashion ... and neither are we. More to the point here, our innate learning process is not naturally organized in a cause and effect fashion either. The Universe is a whole-form singularity. While we can apply cause and effect thinking to describe events after the fact, we seldom can do that before the fact.

There is a formal argument for Determinism that challenges the idea that we can apply cause and effect thinking to describe the events in the Universe as we know it. The argument is based on the presumption that we could "if we had all the information required to do so" - i.e.: if we knew everything there was to be known, including what we cannot possibly know before the fact, we could use cause and effect to describe the future of the Universe precisely. This is a fallacious "Philosopher's Argument" for a Universe other than the one we live in, that is perfectly organized to suit the demands of the cause and effect paradigm being used to describe it after the fact. The "Philosopher's Argument" I point to here requires a Universe where everything that can be known, and needs to be known, is known, before the fact in trying to describe what will happen that has not happened yet. That is not the Universe we live in, and believing it is the Universe we inhabit would be one of the most egregious errors of thinking you could possibly make. Making that error you would find yourself living inside of a massive delusion that contained everything else you believed to be true as well.

In this Universe, the one we actually inhabit, there is still a degree of uncertainty, chaos and mystery. At the macro level we can run calculations to send a ship to the moon, but we have to allow for innumerable adjustments that will need to be calculated and re-calculated along the way for that mission to succeed. The initial trajectory we predict is never accurate to fact.

- ✓ After the fact we can explain exactly why our descriptions of how things would be was not accurate, and assume the delusion of explaining things makes them so before the fact as well.

- ✓ Something closer to reality seems to be that we cannot even begin to calculate the cascade of events that occur once we begin making decisions and taking action, and this is compounded and exacerbated when there are others involved making decisions and taking action of their own in parallel to what we are doing.

Scientists cannot yet predict the velocity and the trajectory of a particle at a quantum level, despite the incredible accuracy of the mathematics they have worked out to do so. Even using a supercomputer with superhuman capability to run their calculations scientists remain at a loss to do this seemingly simple thing (as per classical physics' Newtonian mechanical descriptions of the Universe).

"The concept of a path or trajectory plays a central role in our understanding of the motion of objects and fluids. Much like a route traced on a road map, a trajectory tells us where an object started, where it goes, and how it gets there. There may be alternate routes, some more likely than others. Hence, analysis of a set of trajectories provides us with an intuitive tool for understanding possible complex dynamics. Macroscopic objects obey Newtons equation of motion, $m\ddot{q} = f(q(t))$, where q is the position of the particle at time t and $f(q(t))$ is the force acting on it. Given values for both position and velocity at time t, we can compute the trajectory that the object will follow and as a result, we can predict with certainty where the object will wind up. However, at the atomic and molecular level where objects obey the rules of quantum mechanics, Newtons equations of motion are no longer strictly valid and the concept of a unique trajectory given a set of initial conditions becomes murky at best. This is because,

CHAPTER FIVE

*fundamentally, quantum mechanics is non-local, an issue to which we will return later. In addition, the Heisenberg uncertainty principle states that when measurements are made, **we cannot simultaneously determine with infinite precision the exact position and velocity of a quantum particle, although in principle this is possible in Newtonian mechanics**. Consequently, it seems as though we cannot speak in terms of the unique trajectory followed by a quantum mechanical object."*

From: **Quantum Mechanics with Trajectories: Quantum Trajectories and Adaptive Grids** - Robert E. Wyatt, Department of Chemistry and Biochemistry, University of Texas, Austin, Texas and Eric R. Bittner, Department of Chemistry and Center for Materials Chemistry, University of Houston, Houston, Texas - February 7, 2003

(**Author's Note:** *Emphasis in the quote above is mine*. Even scientists resort to using the language, "*... **we cannot simultaneously determine with infinite precision the exact position and velocity of a quantum particle, although in principle this is possible in Newtonian mechanics**,*" when speaking about predicability - i.e.: perfect cause and effect prediction is not an absolute in science, but suggests at best a logical possibility.)

The illusion that we can predict things in a cause and effect manner, BEFORE THE FACT, is delusional. We run that particular delusion after the fact more often than not, because the bad learning we have had taught us to think in cause and effect terms by default. The most important point to get about the natural organization of the Universe as a whole-form entity is that only after the fact ... i.e.: after an event has occurred ... can you dissect the event to reveal what happened in a causal, sequential, linear, step-by-step fashion. As the event is unfolding it is virtually impossible to predict with perfect accuracy what will happen, when it will happen, or why it will happen, in the real-time context. The impossibility of perfect prediction is especially evident in virtually all things human, including the unique dynamics of human relationships, affairs and interactions.

> ✓ **While we cannot begin to calculate the cascade of events that may occur, or the unknowns in any given**

system, or predict our way out of uncertainty or chaos, we may be able to better prepare ourselves for it when it happens.

- ✓ However, least I leave you to assume otherwise, unpredictability is not at all bad, e.g: it makes games, sporting events and even watching things like nature documentaries and reality television exciting, if all the events of our lives were perfectly predictable no one would be interested in them.

"The Game Is Afoot"

From the first three-day workshop I attended with Roye, the next couple of years flew by for me. I continued to sit in rapture when a bit of magic was being performed in front of me, and there were times I believed it was a show put on for my unique and particular benefit. I felt like Dr. Watson being trained and drilled in the art and science of observation and deduction by Sherlock Holmes. In my case it was Roye who was doing the training and drilling as I gained skill, and it included the art and science of induction and adumbration as well. The entire experience was like playing a real-life game, where the stakes were incredibly high, as was the reward. I was committed as could be, and in the game for life.

It was in part the unpredictability about what would happen next that made sitting in the room and learning with Roye, so captivating. Not knowing exactly what was going on at any moment drew me even further into the matrix of the game I was engaged in with him. My lack of ability to predict the outcome of each workshop, including knowing what I would get from it, made showing up again and again worthwhile. Without the factor of 'not knowing' my attention and interest would have faded away long before I could have learned what I had come to learn. The concept and experience of 'not knowing' is so important to the structure of learning, games and life that I would say with confidence they are not really possible to do well without it.

CHAPTER FIVE

I remember clearly the video games that were beginning to become extremely popular when my son was young. The earliest games were mostly amusing because you could interact with the movement on a screen to make something happen - something remarkably innovative at that time. The newest games draw you into a film like experience where you become a first-person active player in the drama as it unfolds.

I watched the development of video game technology evolving from the first generation of the computing paleolithic age of 2-D, single color, line drawing based games like "Pong" and "Asteroids" slowly progress through 2-D, multi-color, simple graphical animations like "Centipede" and from there move through the early stages of second generation, second-person, full color, character animation games like "Pac-Man" and "Kong" to full-fledged third-generation, first-person, 3-D cinemagraphic gaming like "Halo" and "Call of Duty."

Games went from being simple on-screen line graphics that could be controlled with strokes on a keyboard, to sophisticated, detailed graphical stories, however what remained the same is that what keeps players coming back was the unknown. What they cannot predict before it happens, and figuring out ways to deal with what they have encountered that has stopped them in the past, becomes the reward for continuing to play. As soon as the game becomes predictable it becomes boring and no longer interesting to the player.

Advanced gaming designers, using a deep understanding of human patterns of learning based in some of the latest scientific findings and thinking, found ways to delay the effect of boredom setting in too soon. One way they addressed it was by segmenting the game into "levels" with each level becoming progressively more difficult to figure out. This approach satisfies the basic learning pattern installed for many players during early childhood experiences, especially those installed in school, i.e.: the players expect separation between levels of learning and a linear sequential progression to the learning.

Video game players are also rewarded as they complete and master each level in the gaming experience. There is a deeply ingrained expectation of learning sequentially and experiencing pleasure in mastering the levels of learning as they are presented. This matches the earliest learning experiences of game players as well, i.e.: getting the "gold star" from the teacher for doing what they were told, and being a good boy or a good girl from their nursery, pre-school days.

Let us call this the "Gold Star Effect."

The Gold Star Effect keeps video game players coming back for the next gold star, or its equivalent. In video gaming it is bells, whistles, bright lights and keeping score. The Gold Star Effect also keeps people slaving at work they dislike or hate for decades by the use of rewards like "promotions" and "raises." Some sophisticated employers even use the techniques of modern game design to implement the Gold Star Effect and keep employees on the hook. Marketers, especially those that are primarily Internet based extensively use what gaming designers have incorporated from psychology, anthropology, game theory, behavioral economics and neuro-economics in their approach to wooing consumers. Modern politicians keep teams of highly paid consultants from these disciplines on full-time retainer to advise them for the same effect.

The Gold Star Effect pattern works best after people have been deeply conditioned to defer the meting out of the rewards they earn to the whims and agendas of others who control the rewards. People who have been conditioned in this way, usually beginning in early schooling or before that in the home, continue to respond within the boundaries of this learned pattern. On the other hand, people who have broken free of the Gold Star Effect pattern, who are able to validate and reward themselves, become much more self-directed in their behaviors.

People who eschew the rewards they earn being in the control of others are far less susceptible to the Gold Star Effect. Some newer video game players have become less susceptible to the Gold Star Effect, especially when it is blatantly used in a "flat" environment, e.g.: in a linear, sequential, step-by-step pattern within progressively more challenging levels of a game. This is true for a number of different reasons including recognition and deep familiarity with the pattern.

The Gold Star Effect works as well as it does, where it does, precisely because it remains largely out of awareness.

In a "flat" video game environment each time the player encounters the same level of play in the game they are presented with the same scenario and the same options to surmount the challenge being posed. This kind of clear sequential, linear, cause and effect learning works well at a basic level for a period of time, provided the right rewards are offered. After enough exposure this kind of repetitious learning environment becomes boring, hence the need for a new generation of video gaming. One response has been to use "fuzzy logic" to make gaming more interesting.

Fuzzy logic is what makes life inherently interesting. Where traditional logic deals with truth statements as absolutes, using a binary model of "true" and "false" … either/or, with no grey space. Fuzzy logic also deals with truth statements, but with the potential for significant grey space. It does this by adding in the notion of partial truth. In fuzzy logic there are limits of truth, possibilities of truth, probabilities of truth and even statements that are both true and not true simultaneously.

Essentially we move through life using fuzzy logic as we decide a myriad of things from how to get to where we are going, to what to eat. Life as we actually experience it seldom presents itself as absolutely true or false, e.g.: "Is it better to take the longer scenic route or the shorter, more direct route using the highway?" or "Is chocolate ice cream better (or worse) than vanilla ice cream?" Resolving decisions like this often demands that you apply fuzzy logic, considering the consequence of each option in the moment without any expectation of true or false in the comparison.

On one day the answer may be that we want to enjoy the scenery on the long route, and on another we are more interested in getting there. Or maybe the decision about which route to take is based on our expectation about how much traffic there will be on the highway. We do this without having any way of knowing how much traffic there is, and relying on our best guess instead. The decision about chocolate or vanilla may be dependent on your mood, or maybe what you having with it, that impacts the choice you make. Once again, we do this without access to an absolute value set against which to make the decision.

When you apply fuzzy logic to the gaming environment the choice of what to do with your character changes as the game unfolds. With each choice you make, the game presents you with alternate options. With each option more options become available adding to the complexity and the unpredictability of the game. As the player, you now become an active agent, determining what game you are playing by virtue of the choices you make in an ongoing way. This adds to the sense of empowerment that you have as you engage in playing the game, i.e.: what you do counts beyond absolute success or failure in the moment. Like in real life, what you do now in the game you are playing impacts what options become available to you down the road ... and those that remain available to you as you proceed.

While this may seem deterministic in a video game, and to a great extent is because of the finite nature of the game's programming, in real life the limits of possibility are much more extensive. From a human perspective, even if the limits of possibility in real life are finite they seem infinite in terms of our ability to calculate them with certainty. It often seems to us like our future is determined by our past actions, and yet this may not be true. If it were true that our future is purely determined by our past actions, there still is no way we have to calculate the outcomes of our actions with absolute certainty.

In many work scenarios the Gold Star Effect remains largely out of conscious awareness by virtue of the distance between the action taken and reward received. The lack of an absolute, perfect one to one relationship between action taken and the guarantee of receiving the reward keeps the "player" (in this case the worker/employee) guessing about how the system works. When a player deduces a hidden set of rules to the game, for which they will be rewarded, they become motivated to play the game. In the work environment this naturally plays into the hands of employers because events continue to unfold that are subject to change. An employer does not even have to design "the game of work" to be interesting. The "game of work" will be interesting by virtue of the multi-level, multi-layered, multi-player, multi-contextual environment that the game is played in, which is in itself chaotic.

By the time an employee gets to the employer they have been deeply conditioned to play the game, and to look for and accept the rewards offered. A typical scenario might be someone who gets a good salary that lets them buy the material goods and experiences they think will bring them comfort and satisfaction, and the illusion of (financial) safety. Familiarity with this scenario was installed long before the "game of work" began for the player, going from being taken care of by their parents, to being taken care of by the system, i.e.: school, the company, the government ... or whatever pseudo parent steps up to "care" and "provide" for them. The key to keeping the system going is always having a substitute for a warm teat available to offer comfort, sustenance and safety to the players.

Seeing Beyond Illusion

I remember sitting in the room for countless hours with Roye mesmerized by the unpredictability of what he was doing. When I first began learning from Roye, I was utterly incapable of picking out the path he was on when he worked with people. It was like reading a brilliant mystery novel or watching a great detective film. Part of what kept me coming back was trying to figure out the ending by the clues that appeared along the way ... before the actual ending was revealed.

The concept of discovery was present for me in the early years of my learning with Roye. NLP and hypnosis are mysterious to outsiders to begin with, although they are much less so almost as soon as someone pulls back the curtain, even a little. The entire subject of non-verbal communication is the same ... from what some people refer to as "body language," to the esoteric art of "facial emotion recognition," and onto even more obtuse domains like "human interactional dynamics" - they all share a kind of impenetrable barrier to common observation and understanding, except to devout insiders. The impenetrability of non-verbal communication remains present for most people despite our innate, intuitive recognition of the process. Yet there was a definite thrill in exploring the unknown, especially when the promise of becoming enlightened beckons - or maybe I should specifically say there definitely was for me.

As I continued to learn it became more and more apparent what to pay attention to and what was background noise when Roye was engaged in communication with clients. Once I had begun to get it I could see how the concept of background noise in communication and interaction generalized beyond the work I was learning to do with Roye. Observing Roye's mastery with clients was coupled with a yearning for and expectation of developing that mastery myself. From the start, it became apparent that knowing what to attend to and not, separating the signal from the noise, was crucial to gaining competence in the art and science I was learning. In human interaction and communication there is just too much information to track all of it well, you must learn to divide and direct your attention to what is most important.

Mastering non-verbal acuity ... noticing, recognizing and unraveling non-verbal signals ... is the first step in mastering non-verbal communication. Noticing ... or mindfully perceiving, comes before the act of sense or meaning making, and well before becoming able to intentionally respond. The key to mastering non-verbal acuity begins with learning how to divide your attention between what is in the background ('ground') and what is in the foreground ('figure'). The idea of figure and ground comes from my years in architecture as a student and practitioner, before becoming an adjunct professor teaching the concept to students of my own who would themselves become practitioners. The concept is an aesthetic way of perceiving that served me in ways I had not fathomed my training as an aesthete would those many years before I found myself sitting at the knee of the master learning once again a new form of art.

Most of what people do is track just in the foreground, or the figure, in communication, i.e.: the words that connect and link ideas. The words are not the ideas themselves, just the part of the language people use to access and surround their ideas. Yet some of the words people use are critical to the ideas they are trying to express, including the way they "language" them. The way people express themselves ... the way they language their ideas, the specific words, sequencing and presentation they choose ... how that points to something about them as the chooser of that particular way of making themselves known, versus other ways that could have been chosen ... forms the ground of communication ... and yet, this most critical observation remains in the background and out of sight for most listeners..

In the unique language used to express an idea, i.e.: beyond the idea that the words explicitly state, what words alone can never say becomes available, and even apparent, to a trained observer. Things like speaker bias, what they have and have not included in what they are saying, are there for someone tracking both the words and the languaging of a speaker as they share their ideas. In any live interaction there are many non-verbal cues simultaneously present in addition to the specific language used ... tone, emphasis, expression, gesture, posture, movement, distance, angle and speed of approach to name a few of the more obvious ones. Roye was a master of the art and science of observation, i.e.: non-

CHAPTER FIVE

verbal acuity, as well as a masterful communicator when he was the speaker.

One day I asked Roye about something he had done with a client, a particular gesture he was fond of using. It was an elegant movement of his right hand; a movement of his hand simultaneously away from his body and forward, as he swung it outwards to the side and rotated his hand over itself in a spiral gesture, often leaning his torso forward or back as well as he gestured. He often used this quite particular movement when he was leading someone to consider their internal experience. What I noticed was the remarkably hypnotic response it provoked when he did it.

At first I thought the spiraling hand gesture that Roye used was hypnotic in and of itself. I asked Roye to "teach me how to do it" and he agreed. Each time Roye would ask me "What do you want?" as I attended workshops with him week after week after that I would ask for the same thing, "Teach me how you do that thing with your hand," and he would agree. This went on for months, and I became exasperated with him, believing he was hiding the secret from me. Relentlessly I kept showing up and kept asking for the same thing, "Show me how you do that thing with your hand," and he kept agreeing. Despite agreeing and seeming to be on the same page about it, I had become no better at using the gesture when working with "clients" in the exercises we were given than before I had begun asking.

Right around the time I had gotten frustrated enough to consider giving up on ever getting what it was that Roye was doing, something happened and I got "IT" ... there was nothing at all magical about what he was doing with his hand. The "magic" was in two things that occurred around what he was doing with his hand - 1) when he chose to do it and 2) what he said as he did. A third thing about that particular movement that made the entire action so powerful was that it was hypnotic ... graceful and pleasing to watch, and as such it anchored the experience that surrounded it. The gesture was a magician's ploy, a trick or misdirection of sorts, that simultaneously distracted the client's attention for an instant and also anchored them to the suggestion.

It took me a few years to become adept enough myself to begin to recognize the patterns that Roye was noticing and responding to, and what he did in response as he worked with clients ... like the specifics surrounding the spiraling gesture he kept making. I was on my way once I had broken the code of how to pay attention.

BRILLIANT STUFF THIS!!!

After months of relentlessly sticking with it to get Roye's spiral hand gesturing "trick" down for myself I started to pay attention to things differently. I learned to focus on what was happening that I could perceive and notice, and what had to be happening that I could not perceive or notice simultaneously. It was about this time that I developed what I now think of as **The Ultimate Meta-Model Question: "What has to be true for THAT to be true?"** The Meta-Model in NLP is a way to use language to get beneath the surface structure of language that is in the open and obvious. The Ultimate Meta-Model Question became for me a short cut to get there as quickly as possible, without using a step-by-step, cause and effect linguistic modeling process.

A Note On The Outer Limits of Observational Reality

When we return to what we currently know about quantum mechanics at a quantum level we find that there may be no historical determinism outside of the observer's acuity and position the observer chooses, something we might call **"Observational Reality."**

If we apply the concept of observational reality to the considerations of our life, we will find frequent counter-examples of historical determinism. I can point to the effect of Observational Reality in my life. When I first decided to train with Roye instead of the future unfolding as I expected from the actions I had taken ... I thought I was there to complete the process of getting certified as an NLP Trainer as quickly as possible ... something utterly unexpected occurred. From the start I found I was up against the limits of who I thought I was, who I had been trained to believe I was, and living up to the general rule, "Be Good and Fit In." In order to continue I needed to expand the boundaries of my holy quest, the sacred journey, I had begun to "find myself." The story I had constructed to contain the life I was living was no longer big enough to contain me ... it had begun to constrain me instead.

Chapter Six:
Soul Relief

"Many young men started down a false path to their true destiny. Time and fortune usually set them aright."
- Mario Puzo
The Godfather

CHAPTER SIX

Growing Up "Italian"

When I went to begin my training with Roye I had a strong expectation that I would study with him for a year, or maybe two, get certified as a NLP Master Practitioner and then as a Trainer. There was no way I could have known that I would spend seven years apprenticing intensely with Roye. When I look back on that experience now I know with as much certainty as I can that who I was when I drove down to the "Blue Dell Farm" in Pemberton that first time was not who I was when I stopped working formally with Roye seven years later.

If I had been who I was when I decided to continue my NLP training, found Roye, and signed up for the first workshop, I would never have chosen to apprentice with him ... nor would he have allowed the person I was then to become an apprentice of his. Over the course of the first couple of years of studying with Roye a shift began to happen in "who I was" ... and the possibility of something that would not have been possible for "who I had been" emerged. Although it was the first time I was aware that something profound was shifting within me, it was not the first time it had happened. Unbeknownst to me then, I was beginning to resolve my ontological longing. Heck, back then not only did I not know what ontological longing was, I did not even know that it was something ... it simply did not exist.

I now know that the first ontological shift I experienced had happened long before ... sometime between my early childhood and my becoming an adolescent. I lost my way in my middle childhood years. Without any direct proof as I think about it in retrospect it seems the world imposed itself on me when I was a child, and the effect was to lead me away from myself. I got the message that just being "who I was" prevented me from fitting in and compromised my future too. I was being prepared for a future that I could "fit" into, whether or not that was a "fit" for me. Before I could think for myself others had begun thinking for me and deciding what my future should be ... I was in the process of being "made fit" for it. By the way, none of this was malicious, in fact the people orchestrating my future were trying to be benevolent.

Most young people find themselves up against the experience of being led away from themselves. In order for society to work the way it does, it must prepare its young to fit into the way it is designed, i.e.: "as it is." Society must subdue the innate nature of its young, and replace that nature with a way of being that suits society. This requires the members of society to conform to the roles most needed and desired to fulfill its outcomes, not those that are most important to the individual. Pointing to the "greater good" is one of the main means of getting people to sacrifice themselves, without ever allowing them to consider what they are doing or why.

Left to themselves, children are innately pulled in a direction that suits them. Following their innate pull tends to produce individuals who are internally motivated, i.e.: self-referencing and self-organizing, and at the same time very externally directed. These individuals who are internally motivated and externally directed do not fit well into the roles designed for them by others.

Given its druthers, society would likely choose its citizens to be motivated to suit the demands of the environment and times. Such individuals would be externally referenced and organized to create the outcomes of society (not their own), and they would seek to change themselves to "fit in" (rather than seeking new ways to creatively respond so they could remain and continue becoming themselves despite environmental demands or the stimuli present in the moment).

The more individuals are externally referenced and allow themselves to be fit into the external organization of society, the better it is for the "greater good" they have been pointed towards serving. Long before most children have a chance to fully realize themselves, who they are innately has become diverted and compromised. The compromise foisted on our children is done to fulfill the outcomes of the greater good that society has decided they should serve.

The result of this sacrifice is an inexplicable ontological longing. Others have called it, "selling your soul," and I think that too is appropriate. It is a devil's bargain, i.e.: no bargain at all. It was the place I was in when I began studying with Roye at the Blue Dell Farm Hypnotorium … although I had no idea that was true back then. For the first few years, time after time, I showed up for Roye's workshops, compelled beyond reason to return.

CHAPTER SIX

I was convinced, or I had convinced myself, that I was showing up at the Hypnotorium simply to learn NLP. I was there to get certified and get on with it. Running the rat race was what I had been trained to do. Although I did not know it, my soul knew that "getting on with it" was just the excuse I needed to get myself back to study with Roye again and again, despite my frustration at not "getting on with it" as I had planned to at the start.

What I truly wanted from Roye and my time in the Hypnotorium was to regain what I had given up of my own free will ... my soul, or my soulfulness.

My desire to regain my soulfulness remained, despite the fact that I had been inadvertently sold out by those I trusted most. No one meant to sell me out, I was not sold out maliciously. The process was innocuous, as simple as "fitting in" and "going with the flow." It is just what parents have been trained and encouraged to do with their children. Parents are taught their job is getting their children to "Be Good and Fit In." Even parents who believe they are providing an "alternate" route more often than not lead their children to the same place ... selling their souls to get on with it. All in the name of being good parents raising good children, both of whom are and will be primarily judged by how well they fit in and get on with it.

Getting on with it shows up in many different ways, each distinct and yet the same. The pursuit of grades or simply doing well in school is one way. Even when doing well is measured without grading students they experience the grading process. Children instinctively know which ones among them are doing the best work in class, which ones are the teacher's or the coach's pets. Maybe the greatest joke of all is the teacher or coach who truly believes they treat all their children in the same way, i.e.: fairly and equally ... while in reality they may judge all their children "fit," they judge some just a bit more fit than others.

Some children compete and excel (or fail) athletically, others complete in the arena of academics, and some others experience competition in the social arena. Most children experience competitiveness in each of these ways to one degree or another, always trying to find their way to "fit in" regardless of where or how they excel or fail. And their experience of not fitting in is exasperated by the adults around them who cannot, or will not, see the way it affects them.

The process of pursuing "acceptance" continues as children strive to be formally "accepted" as students at the college or university level. Once again when these students graduate, and begin applying for jobs and getting offers from employers, they are striving to be chosen and accepted based on what is often an obscure, obtuse, impenetrable grading system, built on how well they have fit in and how likely it is they will continue to do so. It does not really matter how it shows up, "getting on with it" is the game being taught and played before most of us are ever aware we in a game at all. At every stage of the game, we continue to driven by the Gold Star Effect that began in or before Kindergarten. Now, however, the stakes seem higher as shiny paper Gold Stars are replaced, first by acceptance to and graduation from a prestigious institute of higher learning, and then receiving desirable job offers, to salaries, bonuses and promotions.

Like many Americans of my generation I was a child of immigrants. In my particular case a generation removed from my grandparents homeland of Italy. Yet despite the fact that my parents and all my aunts and uncles were born in the United States, my family was still very Italian culturally. What this meant for us as Americans was that outside the home we would assimilate into the new culture of America … we would fit in. This was part of the deal my grandparents and parents made with their new country … inside the home we would behave much like an Italian family, and outside the home we would fit into the American culture for all we were worth.

Living with two different cultural lifestyles simultaneously created conflict. The invisible question "Where do I belong?" was ubiquitously omnipresent. The question inevitably associated with that question was, "Who am I?" … internally cogitated as "Am I supposed to be an Italian, or an American?" In the United States we handle this by creating morphed labels like, "Italian-American" denoting both our roots and our current status. This solution means we never have to choose, we can be both. While it is a handy solution, it is also crazy making at some level as well.

I grew up trying to fully satisfy both the demands of being 'an Italian' and 'an American'. It was a subtle as the Sunday ritual of making and eating "gravy and macaroni" ("sauce and pasta" for everyone other

CHAPTER SIX

than the Italian-Americans I grew up with, and others like us). Often these meals would include ten, twenty or more family members ... grandparents, aunts, uncles, cousins ... cousins of cousins, etc. Then after dinner my father and uncles would watch NFL football, or MLB baseball ... a very un-Italian thing to do.

During the week I would be eating hamburgers and french fries for lunch at school like my American friends ... and at home for supper we would have things like pasta fagioli (macaroni with beans - one of my father's favorite dishes), eggplant parmigiana, calamari - sometimes fried in a "fritto misto," but more often in a ragu over macaroni when we were following the Roman Catholic tradition of fasting on Fridays. A rarity and one of my personal favorites was "scungilli* fra diavalo" served over some kind of pasta ... usually linguine, spaghetti or capellini (Angel Hair) pasta, or on its own with biscuits of hard bread to soak up the sauce.

Eating a lot of "macaroni" is big in Italian-American families, especially if your family was originally from Southern Italy ... not so much for my "American" friends as I was growing up, who would show up way more often at my house for dinner than I ever did at theirs.

By the response I got when I brought friends home for dinner I knew that they were not eating like we did in their own homes. Almost always it was one of two responses:

a) Absolute delight about what my mother was serving that evening, like when she made macaroni with gravy (although my friends always called it spaghetti and meatballs, regardless of the kind of pasta my mother had made and the plethora of different meats she had cooked in the tomato sauce to make "gravy")

-or-

b) Utter disgust when my mother had made something like calamari or scungilli ... or worst when she was serving organ meats like liver, heart or lungs sauteed and finished in tomato sauce (when I was a kid, to most of my American, i.e.: non-Italian-American, friends calamari and scugilli were fish bait at best ... and offal was for making animal food ... and they were sure neither were fit for human consumption)

AUTHOR'S NOTE: *Unlike some of my childhood friends, one of the direct results of growing up as an Italian-American is that today I can eat almost any food on the planet, especially if it is finished in tomato sauce. That's absolutely true if it is been fried first, then covered with tomato sauce, with cheese ... ideally both mozzarella and parmigiana ... and baked. I am typically ready to give foods are not covered in tomato sauce a try, even when they are among the most unusual and exotic ethnic specialties ... except chicken feet. I do not like chicken feet, and I do not care how you prepared them, even baked with tomato sauce and cheese.*

*Scungilli - rhymes with "surreally" - it is a word in Southern Italian dialect used for "scuncigli" the plural of "scunciglio," the proper Italian word for conch, a popular Italian shellfish cooked in many ways, including in tomato sauce like calamari, i.e.: squid, or marinated and made into a kind of seafood salad.

Early Mis-Education

While at home with my family we keep many of the traditions familiar to Italian families, outside the home we were expected to behave like "normal Americans" and fit in. In some ways, this was especially true in school, where we were told to "pay attention to the teacher, follow the rules, don't make any trouble, get good grades and be good." Some of these demands were easier for me to fulfill than others. I was always a good student and getting good grades came easily to me. Paying attention to the teacher, following the rules and not making trouble seemed more challenging. The conflict became especially significant for me with the idea of "being good."

I thought I was "good," despite the fact that I was not necessarily paying attention to the teacher, following the rules and even when I was making "trouble" (as my teachers, and then the school principal, labeled trouble at least). Being good felt more like a character trait ... first an attitude and then a behavior, like honor or loyalty. I really was kind and thoughtful towards others almost all the time, and I took that as the basis of what it meant to be good.

I was prone to daydreaming or doing something other than paying attention to the teacher when I got bored in class. When some of my teachers noticed me not paying attention they seemed to take a certain pleasure in calling on me so I would stumble over the question

CHAPTER SIX

they asked. If I happened to catch the question and answer correctly when they had caught me daydreaming it just seemed to frustrate them. Either way I would be punished. I probably spent a ratio of about one hour in detention to every four or five days I spent in class in elementary school.

Following the rules was worse for me, as I thought many of them were ridiculous, even as a child. "Why do I have to draw within the lines?" ... "Why do the hearts on the Valentine's Days' cards have to be red??" ... and, "Why can't I glue the blocks together to make the tower taller???" These were just some of things I purposefully did (or did not) that that got me in trouble in school as early as in Kindergarten, and caused me to have to ask these kinds of questions of my teacher.

In every year of my elementary education two things were true because I was not so "good" at following the rules, 1) my mother met every teacher I had from Kindergarten to Eighth Grade, often with the school principal in attendance, for a "Parent-Teacher Conference" about their wanton child's behavior in class (or out of it), and 2) every year I was evaluated by the school psychologist. Depending on the demeanor of the psychologist who was doing the evaluating that year they either threw me out of the evaluation in frustration, or threw me out of it laughing. Neither of these results left my parents laughing however.

Over time I learned I had to "prove myself" - which in translation I now know means I had to justify my existence to those in authority because I had been deemed a "trouble maker" and "trouble makers are no good." The message I got was that as far as the school system was concerned I was "no good." My saving grace was that I was a "good student" meaning I got good grades despite my "poor" behavior. I also got along well with everyone and had a lot of friends, including all the really smart kids and the worst troublemakers. For my teachers this was disturbing, because it meant I could not be all bad ... and they did not really have a category that made dealing with me easy for them.

Bad kids, those who were intractable (uneducatable), were easy enough to deal with because they fit into a nice, neat category. Suppress them in class, and get them through school, so you can get rid of them. These were the ones who would never turn out well or do anything worthwhile as far as the educational system was concerned. Good kids, those who followed the rules and did well in class, were also easy to handle ... bring them up front, use them as an example for the rest of the class and graduate them with honors. The good kids were the stars who would go onto good schools, continuing to get good grades, graduate with honors, get good jobs and continue satisfying the roles they had shown themselves so capable of adopting ... roles that served both themselves and the greater good ... along with "following the rules" and "fitting in" well to the system.

Kids who were like me in school, bright and capable students, who constitutionally were either unable or refused to follow the rules, were trouble all around ... for teachers, for the administration, and often for our parents who also do not know how to handle us. Heck we were the children who did "horrible" things ... like talking to other children, wanting to play more than learn when we were young, asking questions instead of mutely accepting the teacher's pronouncements and worse of all ... not sitting still on our chairs, behind our desks, quietly doing our work for six hours a day at six years old!

On the one hand we ... the "horrible" children ... seemed like we had something to offer and on the other hand, because we are not able or willing to conform, we seemed like we were going to continue to rock the boat and cause trouble. This created a conflicted message in an ongoing way, something like, "You have so much potential ... if only you would learn to do what you are told ... you could be something."

Translated the standard message in the classroom to the "horrible" children sounds like: "Until you give up your individual mind, thinking for yourself and your unique ways of seeing the world, and simply accept the group mind, thinking like everyone else does and follow our way of seeing the world, you will always be good for nothing."

What a message to give a kid, i.e.: "Unless you start accepting your place in the system just like everyone else you'll be good for nothing." ... especially a bright one who can "hear" what is not being spoken!!!

This message is ancient, despite getting updated continuously. In the past it was installed in children's psyches simply as matter of "follow the rules or get the rod" maybe best exemplified by the famous Protestant "Christian" parenting dictum, "Spare the rod and spoil the child." ... which was equally carried out by teachers in schools "in loco parentis" extensively, including the many horror stories I heard from friends in Catholic school about nuns, rulers and knuckles.

Today the message about "be the same and not different" gets installed far more subtly, far more deviously and unfortunately far more treacherously. At home, in schools and on sports teams young children are taught that "everyone is special." At home everyone is treated like a prince or princess - and referred to by parents, grandparents and sometimes other family or family friends in that way as well, in school everyone gets the gold star, on sports teams everyone gets a trophy ... effectively eliminating anyone who actually might be special or different in some way that would allow them to stand out.

In the interest of conformity, diversity and tolerance we've eliminated any chance for our young to be outstanding ... cutting off the flower before the tall poppy in the field has chance to grow and disrupt the nice uniform structure of things ... or god forbid, challenge the system and the status quo. Society has always chosen the preference for comfort and familiarity leading to mediocrity rather than encouraging the kind of peaceable, constructive dissent that leads to disruption, innovation and excellence ... especially in our children.

The conflict about who I was supposed to be at home and out in the world, compounded by the conflicted messages I was getting at school, fractured my sense of self ... i.e.: my ontological integrity. Instead of remaining secure both in who I was and how to aim myself into my future, I had conflict. The choice I was presented with was to either give up who I knew myself to be, or to give up having a future according to those entrusted with showing me the way forward.

One of the geniuses of the 20th century, Gregory Bateson, along with his colleagues at the Mental Research Institute in Palo Alto, California (also known more informally as MRI or the Palo Alto Group), followed examples of early developmental mental fracturing and found that in the worst cases it created what they called a "double bind" where the child is, "damned if they do and damned if they don't." According to the theory of mental health put forth by the folks at MRI, the mental fracturing of the double bind could ultimately lead to the severe mental disorder of schizophrenia. Bateson and his colleagues based their science in linguistics and cognitive theory. From my point of view what they had uncovered was a fundamental crack in the ontology of an individual who is forced to decide to be themselves, or become what they are not.

Today I would argue that the ontological crack that the Palo Alto Group discovered and defined linguistically and cognitively as a double-bind, is really a separation between accepting direct sensory experience, and how someone has been taught (by choice or coercion). In the process of being taught they learned to think about what they experience other than as they themselves experience it directly. This is the fundamental "body/mind" split that is so prevalent in modern society, i.e.: a perceived division between Somatic (empirical, sensory-based, embodied) experience and Semantic (abstract, cognitive, ideational) experience.

Splitting our experience into two things, somatic and semantic, when in fact it is one thing, a singularity ... a Soma-Semantic experience in the "bodymind" or "body-mind" ... creates an unnatural separation leading to massive, frenetic distress. We experience the distress and the consequences of the body/mind split personally as individuals and systemically in society.

Most people manage the distress generated by splitting the body/mind into two separate things by distraction, e.g.: addictions like smoking, overeating, sex, gambling, alcohol or drugs. Some look to the distraction of entertainment, making things like television, film, video gaming, social media and amusement/theme parks multi-billion dollar industries. Virtually all other approaches either create, or attempt to create, coping mechanisms to manage the distress, e.g.: most psychological interventions. At best these interventions provide a means to dull the distress, e.g.: most pharmaceutical interventions.

Modernity unnaturally favors the mind as superior to and dominant over the body, leading to educational systems that attend to our intellectual experience at the cost of our sensory and somatic experiences. Children, left to their own devices, would be outside running, jumping, climbing and swimming at every chance. Yet they are forced to sit quietly in a room absorbing intellectual abstractions spewed at them from the front of the room by experts. They are taught literally, contextually and figuratively that they are to focus on learning how to absorb information and ready themselves to regurgitate it on command. The better they are at absorbing and regurgitating the information presented, the higher the recognition and rewards they receive. This is an unnatural learning process to undergo, and to become fully human again it must at some point be undone.

We have begun to remove the "humanities" from our childhood educational curriculums, to provide more time and space for more mechanistic, technical subjects to prepare our young to undertake further education that is even more mechanistic and technical under the umbrella of programs like S.T.E.M. (science, technology, engineering and mathematics). To create this room we severely diminished or eliminated time and budgets to provide education in the arts and letters that were once considered to be so crucial to becoming fully human, cultured and civil on the way to maturing into an adult who would someday take their place as a contributing member of society, not just a cog in a system designed to produce ever greater productivity and profits.

The antidote to an over intellectualized, mechanistic and technical education is the re-introduction of aesthetics, movement and dialogue in our schools. If we want our future citizens to be civil, cultured and fully human again we must give them the opportunity to encounter what it is that makes us most human, i.e.: not an ability to program and utilize technical devices, but the ability to appreciate the form, smell and wonder of the flowers they encounter. We must teach our children to speak with one another not to one another. We must allow our children to sing and dance ... and learn how to invite others into their revery. This is the offer and promise of substituting whole-form learning for the current rage in subject-based, linear, sequential cause and effect training.

[*Author's Note:* *Only when we as adults regain the ability to stop and wonder at the flowers alongside the side of the road and in the fields, truly speak with one another and not to one another, sing, dance, draw, paint and revel in the joy of life ourselves can we hope to offer this gift to our children and our children's children through them as well.*]

Only by regaining access to whole-form awareness and bringing the system to rest can we hope to provide any permanent relief from the distress installed in us in modern society, including our current educational system. The distress we experience from the unnatural split between body and mind ... leads us away from having the experience of our life as it is happening, in favor of intellectualizing it. We are taught to turn sensation into ideation ... lived experience into abstractions and the representations we substitute for it. We learn to "process" our experiences to project meaning onto them, not to have our experiences directly and perceive meaning based on what we experience as it emerges and unfolds before us.

In not knowing how to have the experience of our life in favor of "processing" our experience, we do not just lose touch with the direct sensation of what is happening as we experience it ... we lose ourselves as well.

Bringing The System To Rest

I came to the Hypnotorium in the early days highly conflicted. I did not have the level of clarity then as I have now. I knew that I was searching for something, but what I thought was missing was a sense of purpose, something I could devote myself to passionately that fit me in my entirety. I was hoping to find a vocation that I would experience as a sacred calling, what some folks might call finding their true purpose. What I was missing though was a sense of myself as a unified being ... whole and complete unto myself. I was lacking in ontological integrity creating the sense of ontological longing I was experiencing. I mistakenly confused ontological longing for existential longing, i.e.: mixing up my desire to know myself as I am, with the desire to find meaning and purpose in my life, especially in my work.

At this point in my life I thought I was perfectly sane, and society told me my perception about my sanity was on the money. Preparing for and then seeking a way to make a good living that is aligned with your interests and what you are good at doing, is a mark of sanity as society defines it. We are not only prepared from the time we are born to make our own way in the world, according to modern social and cultural mores we must find "our purpose" ... the unique thing we were born to be doing, our destiny. I was implicitly taught, like virtually all my peers in any wealthy, privileged, industrialized, first world country on the planet, that finding my "purpose" is a function of doing what I "love" and that it (my purpose) will be directly related to how successful I am at "making money." I was told that one of signs of success at finding my purpose is that I would "do what I love" and then "the money would follow."

"Do What You Love and The Money Will Follow" Translation:

When you know how to parse deep language of this kind of aphorism for the inherent embedded message and suggestion you begin to read: purpose = love = making money, i.e.: purpose = love >>> love = making money >>> purpose = making money. The basic (deep) message about what you were born to do is "making money" ... and the hidden (deep) message is that love = making money, i.e.: your purpose is to do what you love and when you are doing what you love you will be making money, so logically you must therefore love making money!

Growing up a good Catholic boy I also heard all the aphorisms about how "money" was the root of all "evil" ... combine these two concepts (the ancient wisdom about money and evil, and the new age wisdom about money and love) and you get: evil = money = love, i.e.: evil = money >>> money = love >>> evil = love! So the next time you see a phrase like, "All there is is LOVE.", think about what it might really be telling you to believe, and what follows on from there.

Are you at least beginning to see how insidious the messages of society can be yet?

In pre-modern times people had predetermined roles they followed, husband/wife ... father/mother ... solider/serf ... king/peasant ... and most often these roles were handed down from generation to generation. Sons followed their fathers, taking over the farm, learning a craft or begging in the streets. If you were among the few who were noble born your life too was predetermined, but along a different path ... one that is no more necessarily aligned with who you are innately than that of the beggar's son. At least, because these roles were so clearly defined and understood, people found solace in them.

Doing what you are doing and accepting it for what it is, and no more than that ... i.e.: farming makes you a farmer because you are farming, not because G-d destined you to have a farmer's soul ... provides existential peace. Today we are taught in every way that we must find our purpose to experience existential relief, substituting what we do for who we are, as the basis of our being. Depending on how you look at it this is either insanity ... or what must be a leading cause of it.

I now believe that no amount of existential relief would have satisfied me or my need to find myself. If I had not gotten to know Roye and followed the path I did as a result, or another that would have reached the same end, I would still be unsettled and searching today.

I needed to resolve a fundamental question first, "Who am I?" before I could move onto anything purposeful and satisfying in my life.

The process I thought of as "learning NLP" with Roye was the path I was running on, back to myself, to an ontological integrity and to the resolution of my ontological longing.

Today it is clear to me that learning about NLP was not what "saved" me. In those years I did learn enough about NLP and hypnosis to become masterful in applying them, but what "saved" me was the way Roye was applying them with me. More to the point his unique model "The Generative Imprint" using the tools and technology of NLP and hypnosis helped me to find my center, learning to reside there and operate from there into the world-at-large.

A way I like to talk about being at and operating from my center is, "Bringing the system to rest." Being "at rest" refers to the entirety of my experience in the world ... internally, my body-mind experience, and in relation to the system that I am a part of that simultaneously contains me externally. When I am "at rest" I am settled and at ease, without conflict, internally and externally ... simply resting in a "Ready State."

"The Ready State" was a phrase I picked up working with Roye. He used it when he referred to the state he would lead folks to where they are ready for whatever emerges, meaning wherever I am with whomever is present, or if I happen to be alone I remain ready for what comes up, what needs to be done or doing nothing at all (at least in the moment). When I am at rest in the Ready State I can easily take action ... or not,

CHAPTER SIX

there is no hesitation or urgency to act, both are equal and remain fully available based on circumstance and choice.

Learning to access and remain in a Ready State was one of the most powerful outcomes of my years of training with Roye. I know it has changed my life dramatically, and I have seen how it has changed the lives of clients I have worked with over the years as well. The beginning point is somatic integration, becoming aware of what you are experiencing as you are experiencing it, i.e.: awareness that is sensory-based and embodied. This sounds remarkably obvious and simple, and it is once you have learned how to do it. Yet without access to the Ready State being aware of what you are experiencing, as it happens, is somewhere between unlikely and impossible.

Most people "think" they are aware of what is happening as they are having an experience, yet very few are even remotely aware of what is happening as it happens beyond the age of one, or if they were lucky, two or three. It is far more common for people to experience what is happening in terms of what they want or wish it would be, how they know it to be from past experience, or what they are projecting it will be in the future, i.e.: how it should be now, was back then or will be someday.

"Wanting something to be anything other than what it is opens the doorway to misery." - J. Riggio

The skill of remaining present to what is actually happening as it unfolds in real time is so critical to the resolution of ontological longing that there is no other place where you can begin the process. Until the system is at rest it remains virtually impossible to be aware of the experience you are having, as it is happening. Coming to rest requires that you learn to use your body well, first learning to integrate somatic awareness and response. You must be able to recognize what is happening in your embodied experience as it is happening, including how you are responding to it in the instant you begin responding.

Embodied experience includes at least two critical components
...

1. What you are experiencing in your body that is internally generated and/or externally stimulated
2. What your somatic responses are to the internal and external experiences you are having

The combined result of your somatic awareness and somatic responses manifests as your expressed behavior. The most significant thing you can do if you want to live your life in the Ready State - i.e.; experiencing everything fully and remaining ready for anything - is learning to "run your own behavior" intentionally ... intentionality is the key to readiness.

"Run your own behavior" sounds trite ... something almost too simple to mention. However, most people are not even close to being able to run their own behavior. What is far more likely to be true for most people is that they experience something akin to a "life simulation" ... responding to every internal and external stimulus as it occurs firing off their conditioned responses like one of Pavlov's dogs. In fact, the entirety of civilized society demands that you operate based on the responses it has conditioned into you before you had a mind of your own. This is the process of sacrifice that leads to what I am calling "ontological longing" ... or "selling your soul." I am referring to the process of being conditioned to **"Be Good and Fit In"** to what society wants and needs for you to be for the sake of what it calls the greater good.

A large part of the conditioning process that keeps you on track is the Gold Star Effect, i.e.: the promise of the rewards society offers you. Often society does keep its promise, but only after you have denied yourself becoming who you innately are in the service of it. If you simply do what your are told, follow the rules, align yourself with where society tells that you are most needed, do what is most desired, and go along with the powers that be ... you will do just fine. You will get into a good school, you will graduate with honors and get a good job, you will get to live in a nice home, drive a nice car and care for yourself and your family well. If you do what is asked of you society will ensure that you are taken care of ... at least that is the promise. Those who succeed reap the rewards of this promise ... in other words they keep getting one gold star heaped upon another.

CHAPTER SIX

Society plays an unfair game with the gold stars it hands out though by creating artificial scarcity. De Beers, the famous South African diamond mining cartel owned by one family, the Oppenheimers, from the 1920s until 2011 while diamond mining, production and sales were consolidated under their reign, has also been accused of artificially increasing the demand for diamonds. The ploy of releasing only a limited number of diamonds - especially those of the highest quality at any one time - increases the perceived scarcity and value of diamonds, despite whatever the actual supply might be, a supply that had been unilaterally and wholly controlled by De Beers. "Society" has created an artificial scarcity of "gold stars" in much the same way, parsing out the "best" opportunities, and the rewards they carry with them, to only those who play by the rules that society dictates are mandatory if you want access to the very best it (society) has to offer.

When I met Roye I was there myself, following the "company line" chasing the next gold star. Although I had broken some of the rules, and had never really learned how to submit or follow the authorities, I was still fairly conventional. I had figured out a way to get a good job, or at least create one for myself. I was interested in material and social rewards, those that I had learned to strive for and saw others getting. I wanted to be respected and admired. I was a pawn of the society that had raised me. What I was not was "at rest" ... instead I was in a state of distress, tearing apart my life without really understanding what I was doing or why I was doing it. What I was experiencing should be what we consider the basis of insanity, or at least what we call being insane, but instead society tells us it is "normal" to experience this kind and level of distress while we are striving to "find ourselves." The kind of social "distress" I was experiencing is typically referred by another word, "stress" ... as though shortening the linguistic reference makes it more bearable and normal.

Considering social distress, especially ontological and existential distress, as "normal" can only occur in an insane society.

At first I bought the theory that experiencing extreme stress as you make "progress" in your life is normal, and I thought I was sane, or at least as sane as anyone else I knew. Then I began waking up and realized I was truly living an insane life within an insane social model. When I sought relief, I found that all the ordinary physical and/or psychological medical references controlled by the insane society I was living in had to offer me were ways to modulate and cope with the "symptoms" of stress I was experiencing.

I was lost and had no easy or clear way back to sanity on my own. I was caught in the web, but I knew enough to recognize that struggling against it would only ensnare me further. While I did not have a path to freedom yet, I decided that I had to begin to make my moves within the structure of the system without attracting to much undue attention from it. From where I stood it appeared to me that "the only way out was through" ... so I dove in, going deeper, becoming fully present to the insanity I was living.

Fortunately for me, right around the time I realized how "insane" the society I was living in was and where it was leading me, I met someone who recognized the symptoms on my "insanity" for what they were. Even more fortunate for me he had something to offer that went beyond symptomatic relief. Roye offered me something that went beyond a way to settle the "symptoms" of my soul searching ...the ontological crisis I was waking to each day.

Roye offered me a way to grow a new soul, like a phoenix rising from the ashes of my old soul, the one I was born with intact ... and, in doing that how to bring the entirety of my system to rest.

Chapter Seven:

Harnessing Chaos

"The game was created to demonstrate the futility of individual effort."
- Bartholomew, *Rollerball (1975)*

"Ears. Now, they're important, too."
- Jonathan E., *Rollerball (1975)*

NLP And Hypnosis At The Pond

Sometimes it seems to me that one day I just woke up and everything was different ... and in a way, that would be true. The distinction is that from the day I woke up to the next took about seven years or so to unfold. Along the way there were significant leaps forward, moments in time where I could clearly perceive that things had shifted for me. There were also times when it felt like I was utterly stuck ... not making any progress at all. I could live with these plateaus when they came, but what truly sucked were those times where I was sure I was completely lost again ... that I had slipped back to the time before I had first visited the Hypnotorium and met Roye.

For about two years after I first met him, Roye continued to work from the Blue Dell Farm in Pemberton, New Jersey. Then he moved out, for reasons unknown to me at the time, and we began meeting in New York City, in a lovely apartment on the Upper West Side. It had a kind of Zen feel to it. As I understood it the apartment belonged to a wealthy client of Roye's who had loaned, or rented, it to him. Although the time we spent training in New York was well spent, I missed the farm ... the fields, the great pond ... and the dedicated Hypnotorium.

The pond was a remarkable feature of the Blue Dell Farm for me. It was about an acre in size and quite near the front of the property, just opposite the Hypnotorium as you exited the sliding doors off the alcove. The pond was a stone's throw away from the Hypnotorium, separated by a short expanse of grass lined with a few scattered trees. Across the front third of the pond, separating it from the rear two-thirds, was a small wooden footbridge, so you could cross to the other side of the property. I spent hours and hours on that bridge, in my mind it was truly magical!

After Roye had demonstrated something he was teaching he would proclaim, "Go and do the exercise.", meaning that we should figure out what he had just done, and do our best to replicate it. There were times when replicating "the exercise" was a breeze as the demonstration was straight forward, a particular NLP or hypnosis technique that unfolded in what appeared to be a "step-by-step" way. There was always a flip chart in the room with a description of the exercise on it, and when it unfolded in a way that matched the steps on the page it was easy enough to attempt replicating it.

Sometimes Roye would bring someone up front with him, demonstrating an amazing piece of personal work with them in front of the group, combining overt and covert conversational hypnosis, metaphor, allegory, and some NLP techniques thrown in for good measure, before saying, "Go and do the exercise." When this was the case it was almost impossible to know what he was doing, let alone attempting to replicate it … even with the step-by-step layout of the "exercise" on the flip chart page. Despite the complexity of the demonstration and the virtual impossibility of replicating it, Roye would never explicate further. If anyone approached him with a request to "explain the exercise" he would simply tell them to go and do the best they could based on what they thought he had done, or what they thought they saw him doing.

It was my preference if the weather was agreeable to go outside with a partner or two and "do the exercise" on the bridge spanning the pond. There were moments on that bridge that were inexplicable in terms of serendipity. I remember working with someone, "Mark" who began attending some of Roye's workshops after I had begun training with him. We were on the bridge doing an exercise, after I had been training with Roye for almost a year and a half. The exercise was about a particular way of accessing the Ready State using the "iconic, symbolic, representation" of what Roye called the "Generative Imprint" that would emerge in conjunction with a Generalized Desire State experience.

When we are experiencing a specific state, a default experience of that state will be present in sensory terms as well. There will always be both internal sensory representation and external sensory representation, i.e.: what happens when the state experience is present internally and what is happening that you can be aware of externally. Depending on the state, what you become aware of and how you are aware of it shifts. Think of it as a shift in consciousness that flows in conjunction with state, or "state dependent experience." Having both internal and external sensory experience is a given in any state if you are conscious … being aware of internal or external sensory experience is never guaranteed.

The exercise that Mark and I were working on that particular day was to elicit and identify the specific markers of the state dependent experience of the Generalized Desired State, or GDS. By that time in my training with Roye I was already relatively technically skillful. I still had a long way to go to become masterful beyond mere technical proficiency, but I could run exercises fluidly and replicate the outcomes of the demonstration … if I could follow what Roye had done. I was working with Mark on generating conscious awareness of the internal and external sensory experience associated with the states we were eliciting.

If you were sitting on the bridge, watching me run the exercise with Mark, you might think I was using some kind of hypnosis. I would argue that I was not using hypnosis at all, instead I would call what I was doing using "hypnotic protocol" in communication - this is actually a very common thing we do, at least as I define it. My definition of hypnotic protocol is, "Giving someone a clear set of instructions they can and will follow." This is both extremely easy to do, and at the same time requires great skillfulness to do elegantly.

"Giving someone a clear set of instructions they can and will follow.", while extremely straight forward is not necessarily as easy as it sounds. What most folks will do is give someone else a "set of instructions they themselves could and would follow." In other words, most people communicate with others as though they are communicating with themselves and not the person or people with whom they intend to communicate. This alone is responsible for a huge amount of the miscommunication that has occurred throughout the ages, more likely than not starting a few wars. Most assuredly, although I haven't done the research, I'd be willing to bet that miscommunication has been the cause of more than a few divorces and more business failures than most people could possibly imagine.

If you intend on being a skillful communicator you need to learn how to "Give a set of instructions that THE OTHER PERSON can and will follow." There is a trick to communicating well, especially if you intend to use hypnotic protocol as I have defined it, i.e.: "Giving someone a clear set of instructions they can and will follow." The trick to developing skillfulness in using hypnotic protocol in communication is first learning to recognize how you are communicating with yourself. You have to learn to "hear" your own internal communication BEFORE YOU SPEAK IT OUT LOUD … as well as when you speak it out loud. This is the basis of "self-communication."

Depending on how you are organized you will have a preference in the way you communicate with yourself and the kind of representations that you use most often that have the biggest impact on you. You can "speak" to yourself in any sensory form, what NLP refers to as representational modalities ... visual (vision), auditory (hearing), kinesthetic (feeling), olfactory/gustatory (smell/taste) ... or what NLPers call a "four-tuple" (V-A-K-O/G). Just as you have your unique preferences, others you interact with will have theirs as well, and they are highly likely to be different then yours in some way.

I slice the distinction of sensory form a little finer in the MythoSelf Process model than they tend to in NLP, beginning with the same representational modalities, but divided into a "five-tuple" (V-A-K-O-G), where smell (olfactory) and taste (taste) are held as distinct sensory modalities. I also add "vestibular" and "proprioceptive" senses to this list as well ... i.e.: balance and spatial awareness. We could call this a "seven-tuple." The vestibular and proprioceptive senses together, in combination with kinesthetic felt sense, are what I call "somatic awareness" ... and is critical in learning to "hear" yourself.

Somatic awareness includes internal and external references of where your body is in space, what your body is doing and experiencing, and how your body is relative to the space you are occupying, e.g.: how far from other objects you are, the velocity and trajectory of movement relative to other objects including other people in the space, and if you are moving towards or away from them, etc. In my experience we "hear" our body as loudly, or even more loudly, than we hear our voice. I refer to the total communication from our body as "somatic communication," both as body-based feelings and as physical behaviors.

We "hear" our bodies speaking, i.e.: our somatic communication, and we make sense of what our bodies are communicating in a different part of our brain than we use to "hear" the language of our voice. The main part of the brain that makes sense of what our body is communicating is what I refer to as the "Silent Brain" ... technically, the cerebellum. This part of our brain integrates, co-ordinates and helps to control gross body movement such as throwing a baseball or dancing, as well as fine motor movement like plucking a small berry from a branch.

As cognitive scientists and neuroscientists we are also becoming aware of the fact that movement and emotions are deeply connected to one another, e.g.: movement both influences and indicates our emotional state. The "Silent Brain" is also highly connected with our limbic system, the part of our brain that directly organizes our emotional response ... such as the charge we might get from being touched on our own nipple or possibly from touching someone else's ... or maybe just from thinking about doing that now. The entire somatic communication channel is very finely tuned, and very fast to respond to data ... extant as well as imaginal data.

When you become skillful at "hearing" somatic communication ... despite the influence of the specific stimulus you are responding to ... you regain the ability to:

- **Have the experience of your life**
- **Direct your responses, and**
- **Choose the direction you take`**

Once you can hear your own communication, you must learn how to connect it to the response it creates within you ... first and foremost at the somatic level. Your self-communication creates a response in the way you feel in every moment. Following the way your self-communication generates feelings within you, it also creates an urge to respond behaviorally. Your behavioral response to self-communication might be a simple shift in your current train of thought, a subtle adjustment in your body, a full blown frenzy of activity ... or any of an endless range of possible behaviors you are capable of expressing.

Your response to self-communication, first to how it makes you feel and then in your behavioral response, tells you what your communication means to you ... regardless of what you intended it to mean. If you want to run your own life, to ... have the experience of YOUR life ... you must decide to become skillful in "self-communication" so you can begin choosing how you want to feel and respond intentionally. Once you are skillful in this way you will know what to do to produce the results you intend.

However ... how you feel about and respond to your own communication, is not necessarily what it means to anyone else. This is a critical distinction you must make in becoming a skillful communicator ... remember:

**What your communication means to YOU,
is NOT necessarily what it means to anyone else!**

CHAPTER SEVEN

Hypnotic Protocol In Communication

Early on in my NLP training there was an emphasis on developing excellent communication skills. To my way of thinking this is the most powerful benefit of high quality NLP training. I think of NLP first as a powerful communication protocol, about - learning to "run your own brain" as Richard Bandler calls it - and learning to become extremely skillful in external communication with others as well. There are at least two essential aspects to communicating in this way ...

> ✓ **#1 - Learning to notice for "Signals in the System"** - this includes listening to the words spoken if they are there, as well as listening to what is not spoken, but there is much more to it. You must learn to pay attention with all of your senses ... sight, sound, feeling, taste, smell, proprioception, balance ... everything you have. Using your senses well in this way to pick up on what I call, "Signals in the System" requires that you attend to what you're noticing on the outside as well as what you are noticing on the inside, i.e.: your internal response to what is happening on the outside.

There was a movie from the 1970s, **"Rollerball"** (the original, not the remake, with the actors James Caan and John Houseman). The movie takes place sometime in the future (the date given in the movie was 2018 ... conceptually a long time away from 1975, when the movie was released). In that film, the world government has changed such that corporations now rule the world instead of heads of sovereign states. The "Head of State" did not exist as we now think of that role apart from the corporations operating within their boarders.

In "Rollerball," the corporate entities run the world as a de facto government. In that world the influence of the corporations extends to the way people live their lives on a day-by-day basis. Rollerball is a sport the corporations have designed to entertain the masses, while demonstrating the inferiority of the individual - the equivalent of the "bread and circus" the Romans used to keep the masses at bay - i.e.: "take-out food" and "Reality T.V." of today. [N.B.: not a bad conceptual projection in 1975, given the evidence we now have as we are closing in on 2018 writing about it here in 2014.]

James Caan plays "Jonathan E." a superstar athlete who has become a liability from the point of view of corporations that run the world. Jonathan has become bigger than the game of Rollerball, and that is totally unacceptable. The corporations provide all the benefits people earn and receive in the form of "privileges" … the total sum of the quality of life and lifestyle afforded to individuals in that society, the "Gold Stars" handed out in that time and place. Jonathan has all the privileges/gold stars imaginable as a superstar Rollerball player.

Jonathan has beautiful women "assigned" to him, he lives on a beautiful ranch with a beautiful home. He drives the best cars … has the best clothes … eats in the best restaurants … and on and on. Yet there are two things amiss. Some years before where the story begins in the movie, Jonathan has had to sacrifice his wife to a corporate executive, because he wanted to be with her. Despite the fact that she was married to Jonathan, corporate executives always get what they want regardless of the restrictions that would limit anyone else, so she was forced to leave him and become the de facto "property" of the executive. Now adding insult to the previous injury, the corporation wants to force Jonathan out of the only thing he has left to him that he really loves … playing the game.

Early on in the movie we see Jonathan training some new recruits for the team. He is on a knee in front of the new recruits, with some of the older players watching as he is lecturing the new young players. One of the players is a hot shot recruit who considers Jonathan a dinosaur in the game … old and over the hill … and he is ignoring him. Jonathan notices this and challenges him to "take me out." The young buck puts on his gear, strapping his helmet on and takes off around the skating track that rollerball is played on where Jonathan is kneeling and lecturing the group. The new player is working his way around the track, building up speed to "take out" Jonathan; with his back to the track Jonathan goes back to lecturing the group, unconcerned and seemingly ignoring what is happening behind him.

At the last possible moment, just as the new cocky recruit cruising around the Rollerball track is about to slam into him … "taking him out" … Jonathan ducks and the flips the player over his back,

CHAPTER SEVEN

slamming the recruit into the track instantly and unceremoniously. The group looks on to what has just happened as Jonathan demonstrated his extraordinary skill and he points out to them simply that you have to use your ears, as well as your eyes, when you are playing the game.

In "ordinary communication" you have to use your eyes as well as your ears ... and all your other senses ... as well. In the movie Jonathan excels in "Rollerball" in part because of his extraordinary skills in noticing Signals in the System, but also because he puts his attention on the larger system that contains him as the default operating consideration he must live within. To the demise of the character John Houseman plays as the head of the corporation, Jonathan does not allow himself to get caught or "taken out" because he loses his perspective by focusing too narrowly on himself. Instead of getting lost in "the world according to Jonathan" he keeps his attention on the outside, while simultaneously attending to the signals within and fixed on the outcome he intends to create.

I remember the scene with the hot shot, cocky recruit from this cult science fiction/fantasy movie from when I was a sixteen year old kid and I first saw it. I immediately got the point ... **"Pay attention to the world with everything you have at your disposal."** I also got the point that at any given moment more is going on that meets the eye ... ear ... or any one single way of perceiving things. The system is larger than the individuals it contains, and I learned that if I want to be effective at creating the outcomes I intend I better become skillful at attending to the system-at-large as well as the individuals within it ... including what goes on within myself. Along the way I also began to get that the system shapes me, and everyone else it contains. That insight opened my eyes on the outside, and on the inside, to begin considering everything differently than I had before.

> ✓ #2 - **Learning to communicate effectively using the communication style and preferences of others** - while suspending your own preferences. Your own unnoticed preferences and beliefs interferes with perceiving how others communicate. The first step in becoming an effective communicator begins with putting yourself aside while you are gathering information. Step two contains the "magic" of communication and begins when you use what you find out about other people's

preferences as you build your messages. Giving up "your way" of doing it in favor of picking up on "their way" of doing it, always pays off in communicating with others. Their preferences and beliefs are the way they hold the world intact as they know it to be ... what "reality" is for them.

The communication skills that I learned in studying NLP were critical to being able to use what I am calling hypnotic protocol in communication. Over the years I had been studying NLP, both before Roye and with him, I had learned how to do a few critical things that made using hypnotic protocol with others possible for me. By the time I was sitting on a bridge with "Mark" doing the exercise Roye had instructed us to do, I had become skillful in setting aside my own communication preferences. Although I had yet to become as skillful as I eventually would become in setting aside my beliefs, I knew how to elicit someone else's communication style and preferences. I also had learned how to elegantly guide and direction others using their preferences and not my own.

Using what is happening in the moment to lead someone to a specific state experience is a powerful way of communicating skillfully. Just because a state is fully present and embodied, it does not automatically follow that the person experiencing it will be aware of it consciously. All states have a direct sensory experience associated with them, i.e.: distinct internal or external sensations. Bringing what someone is experiencing in real time, as it emerges and becomes evident, into their conscious awareness is another aspect of using hypnotic protocol. However, people often disregard their direct sensory experience in favor of intellectualizing it. Intellectualization removes you from the real time experience of the moment and conceptualizes experience, replacing it with an abstraction about what has happened, could be happening, or will happen. Intellectualizing projects a story on the immediate, embodied, direct sensory experience about the states you access, becoming what they are for you.

CHAPTER SEVEN

Intellectualizing any experience, rather than remaining present to direct sensory experience, generates a projection of the experience.

Projections of an experience are NOT the experience itself, by default they are illusions or hallucinations 'about' experience ... in a worst case scenario they are delusions largely unrelated to the experience itself.

[N.B.: All projections are based in abstraction.]

Abstracting and not remaining present to direct sensory experience, may "nominalize" the experience. Nominalizing an experience begins by labeling it and substituting the word used to label it for the actual experience itself. This makes experiencing, which is always dynamic, into something static. Instead of remaining flowing and resilient, your experience becomes fixed and rigid.

"Nominalizations" prevent us from being free to update to remain present to our experience as it is happening. In nominalizing experiences we act based on pre-conceived notions about what we are experiencing ... our projections, illusions, hallucinations and delusions. Responding appropriately to what is actually unfolding demands that we remain present to our experience.

Nominalizing experience, and responding to the nominalization, instead of responding to emergent, real-time, sensory information as it unfolds, prevents you from having the experience of your life.

Getting stuck in the loop of nominalizing their experiences is what keeps most people stuck in their life, regardless of whether they find themselves stuck professionally, financially, physically, psychologically, in their relationships, or otherwise. Being stuck inside of their projections versus being present to experiences as they are unfolding, prevents the expression of innate creativity. In my many years working with Roye, I found out that the way we communicate with ourselves and others -

semantically using language and somatically in the way we use our bodies - is the key to unlocking our full potential as human beings.

Re-learning how to access the full range of communication, beginning with how I communicate with myself ... i.e.: self-communication ... was one of the many gifts of studying with Roye and learning NLP.

Author's Note: When experience is nominalized by abstracting it to symbolic representation using language, the actual experience the language is pointing to is lost. E.g.: The nominalization "Love" versus the conscious experience of what is happening that inspires the word "Love" to arise in consciousness, i.e.: the experience of loving and begin loved. In this example the actual experience of the act of loving is lost in favor of labeling it "Love." While "Love" remains static, stuck and rigid in noun form, "loving" and "being loved" are active, dynamic verbs. Turning loving and being loved into "Love," is akin to turning ailments and their processes into diagnoses and diseases, instead of addressing the symptoms as part of a larger overall systemic equation. A systemic approach always includes the individual's entire life experience, e.g.: the totality of the behaviors, contexts and situations that they find themselves in and affect them. Thought of in this way ... "Love" is only a symptom or the aftereffect of loving and being loved.

Nominalizations, States, And Magic

One way people miss out on having their life is by creating projections about it instead of experiencing it. By labeling their experience and associating the state more with the label they have given it than the actual sensory experience of it, people begin living in relation to their projections about life and not life itself. For instance people often label states they are experiencing as emotions, e.g.: "happy" ... "sad" ... "glad" ... "grief" ... "excitement" ... "depression" ... blah, blah, blah ... you name the state, you can find someone who will think they have experienced what you have just named. When someone names a state, they are labeling the effect of the state as it affected them, not the process of experiencing the state as an active process. Once you have labeled an active process in this way, i.e.: as a nominalization, accessing and running the process intentionally becomes a distant possibility.

CHAPTER SEVEN

Because most people associate their state experiences with a nominalization instead of the active process most people find that their states run them instead of the other way around. When your states run you, you lose the ability of making choices about intentionally accessing and running your states. The exercise that I ran with Mark, my fellow participant in one of Roye's training weekends on the bridge at the Blue Dell Farm pond in Pemberton, was designed to reverse this situation.

The steps of the exercise we were following were something like the following:

1. Elicit a very powerful resource state, a state in which you felt like you could do anything, i.e.: a Generalized Desired State.
2. Then amplify the state experience so that it was fully present and accessible to the person experiencing it
3. Once the state was fully elicited and present begin demarcating the specific sensory experience

    - First, directing the "client" to become aware of the internal sensory experience of the state, e.g.: what they visualized, heard, felt, tasted and/or smelled internally as the state was being elicited, being amplified and when it was fully present and embodied

    - Next, doing the same with external sensory experience, leading the client to become aware of how they were noticing and processing external sights, sounds, feelings, tastes and/or smells

4. After directing them to notice what they could about their state experience pointing out to the "client" what you noticed for them as you were running the exercise with them, e.g.: what changed that was observable, like how they shifted their bodies ... their posture, their movements, their gestures, their expression ... and more subtle things like how their breathing changed or where

they looked to as you accessed and amplified the state with them

5. Have the "client" run the exercise again from the beginning using all the information they now have explicitly available about the powerfully resourceful state experience they had been having

6. Have the "client" name how they run the state experience with a "code word" that they could use to help them run the experience for themselves ... taking back control of the nominalization that is now associated with the active process and not just the affect of that process

The last step, Step 6, "Have them name the state with a 'code word' that they could use to run the experience for themselves" has a critical distinction built into it. The distinction is naming the active process, i.e.: 'running the state experience' rather than labeling the state and nominalizing it.

When you name an active process and associate the name you have given it the process remains active.

From a neurological point of view referencing an active process represents a critical difference from referencing a static state. Consciously naming a process references the action you took, are taking or need/want to take at some point in the future. This shifts your focus and attention from experiencing the affect of the state to the process of what happens that creates the affect you are experiencing. It would be appropriate to think of this as de-nominalizing.

When you de-nominalize experiencing the state of "Love" it shifts your attention from being stuck in and/or at the affect of "Love" to what happens that creates the experience you call "Love" ... i.e.: what happens at the level of your internal sensory experience, e.g.: what do you feel specifically and where do you feel it in your body ... "warmth and a pleasant buzzing vibration in my chest" ... and at the level of external sensory experience ... e.g.: how do things look or sound to you when you're experiencing loving or being loved ... "things looks softer and more beautiful to me"

CHAPTER SEVEN

Neurologically we cannot run static states, e.g.: "love." However, we can run an active process like, "loving." Whether we externally express the behaviors we associate with "loving" or we only run them in our imaginations, our system responds in a neurologically complete and appropriate way. Either way we express or imagine a behavior our neuro-musculoskeletal system responds as though we are taking action. Neurologically running a behavior builds new neural pathways or reinforces existing neural pathways, depending on whether or not the pattern is pre-existent in the neurological and musculoskeletal systems. This allows you to run the behavior more efficiently and effectively the next time you access it. This process seems to work equally well when you express the behavior in action or only run it imaginally.

The exercise at the pond was designed to allow the person experiencing it to learn to run the behavior of accessing a powerful resource state reliably ... regardless of the external context, situation or circumstances in which they find themselves. When the exercise was run well, and the person experiencing it really got it, a subtle ontological shift would occur ... movement at the level of being. When you experience accessing a powerful resource state you begin to shift who you are at the level of your personal and social identity.

This kind of shift had a remarkable effect of generalizing in the system. Instead of the symptomatic relief of a "presenting problem," accessing and running this kind of generalized powerful resource state moves someone who experiences it to a position where they were no longer able to access the presenting problem, while they are accessing that state. The powerful resource state and the presenting problem become mutually exclusive, and the individual literally has to choose to experience one or the other, because they cannot experience both simultaneously. When someone knows how to access powerful resource states that supercede the presenting problem it still remains a choice for them to do so, i.e.: they can choose to do "this" or "that" but not both. To NOT have the presenting problem they must choose to have the resource state instead. By default NOT choosing to access the resource state means choosing to have the problem instead, once you know how to do it reliably.

Roye would speak of using the "presenting problem" as a lens through which to access a Generalized Desired State, the GDS in the Generative Imprint model shorthand. Accessing the GDS was at the center of his model of working with clients. Properly accessing and running the GDS generates an operating position where anything the person is capable of becomes possible for them. Sometimes we would refer to this operating position in terms of "being at your best." Roye preferred the term, "Ready State," referring to the idea that accessing and running the GDS would allow you to be ready for anything. I agree with him, Ready State, is a much more descriptive and better name for referring to the operating position associated with the GDS than "being at your best."

The experience of having the GDS elicited and made explicit is extraordinary. When the GDS is running, it literally feels like anything is possible, and the lens of consideration becomes focused on possibilities. It may have been the shift created by accessing and running it, or it may just have been coincidence, but sitting on the bridge over the pond at the Blue Dell Farm some amazing things happened.

I cannot count the number times I would be working with someone, or someone would be working with me, and some magnificent bird, like a Great Blue Heron, would fly just above our heads before landing directly in front of us in the pond. Other times a Great White Egret would be standing motionless staring into the water before striking at something with blinding speed and a surprisingly loud splash that would totally eclipse anything we had been doing. Yet at other times, a huge C-14 would fly out of nearby McGuire Air Force base low overhead, or a small squadron of F-4s or F-106s would swoop across the sky over the farm, and occasionally we'd even hear the cracking of the sound barrier from a single jet, maybe from a U.S.A.F "Thunderbirds" pilot in an F-14, F-15 or F-16, prior to an air show flying a practice run. The sound of these "birds" obliterating any and all conversation for what was probably less than a minute as they passed by nonetheless left a lifelong impression on me.

These events by themselves were spectacular, however what was even more surprising to me was how often these events happened serendipitously in harmony with someone attaining full access to the GDS. In those moments the pond became a magical place to be, and the event we were engaging in at the edge of that rather large and otherwise unremarkable puddle in N.J. became an indelible marker for the work we were doing, as though the two had merged.

CHAPTER SEVEN

In many ways, during those heady first days learning with Roye sitting on the bridge overlooking the pond at the Hypnotorium I often felt like I had crossed some invisible boundary into Tolkien's Middle Earth ... a place beyond ordinary imagination. The entire Blue Dell Farm was imbued with a kind of charmed presence that became amplified for me around the pond. I do not believe that the farm was magical in any way that could not be explained. I am referring to the position of operating near the edge of ordinary reality, where an expectation of "magic" happening is held. We often had a feeling that we might be about to experience something extraordinary, and often we did. Over my few years at the Blue Dell Farm, "magical" became my ordinary operating position.

The Hypnotorium was at the center of the magical place that was the Blue Dell Farm, and Roye was the magician at the center. Like every good magician Roye had his tricks. One of Roye's "tricks" as that he was a master of "Whole-Form Communication." In the same way I refer to the pattern of integrated Whole-Form Learning or W-learning, a pattern of integrated communication, that I call Whole-Form Communication or W-communication, also exists.

W-communication is a form of multilevel communication, beginning with self-communication. Our self-communication establishes our state experience from which everything we notice follows, i.e.: all of our perceptions, sense making, decision making, behavioral responses, including the overt action we take and the results we produce ... or not. Our ability to experience the world the way we do, and to respond effectively (or not) to the experiences we have, begins with self-communication.

W-communication also includes the way we communicate with others, starting from our ability to have what I've learned to call situational awareness, i.e.: noticing what is happening around us in an emergent manner in real time. When we are situationally aware communicators, we are aware of the external data that is present, as well as the internal data we generate and respond to as part of our experience, i.e.: self-communication. A masterful communicator will be particularly attentive to somatic communication too. Situational awareness provides you with the ability to stay present to what you are experiencing as direct sensory data, to respond to the sensory experience you are having appropriately for what it is, and to refrain from creating abstractions of your experience that exist solely in your mind.

In contrast to operating solipsistically in relation to mental projections, situational awareness requires you to put aside the projections that exist solely in your mind (i.e.: solipsism; the philosophical/epistemological idea that only one's own mind is sure to exist[1]), and to attend to what is extant to your senses empirically (i.e.: empiricism; a theory which states that knowledge comes only or primarily from sensory experience, empiricism emphasizes the role of experience and evidence, especially sensory experience, in the formation of ideas, over the notion of innate ideas or traditions, empiricists may argue however that traditions, or customs, arise due to relations of previous sense experiences[2]). Shifting from a solipsism to an empiricism relative to the data that is present, i.e.: "signals in the system" is the basis for W-communication.

As a multilevel sensorial-cognitive process W-communication extends to the way we communicate with others too. In much the same way that Marshall McLuhan told us "the medium is the message" in W-communication "HOW" someone communicates is as much the message they convey as "WHAT" they communicate literally. In many cases what someone communicates literally is meaningless without considering the structure of how they communicate it. In most cases the "HOW" someone communicates contains more of the meaning than "WHAT" they communicate. W-communication gives you access to the total message being communicated beyond the obvious. Communication in whole-form is the literal expression of the communicator, including the critical aspect of its affect on your own experience.

Another aspect of the multilevel process of W-communication is the consideration of the context in which something is communicated. Context shapes communication as much HOW or WHAT someone expresses. Part of the context is the consideration of "WHO" in communication, e.g.: communication changes based on the relationship of the communicators, whether it is private or public, and whether it is one to one, one to many, or many to many. These are all contextual issues, as are things like the place in which the communication is occurring, e.g.: the same thing said in a pub might mean something very different if it were to spoken in a, classroom, or a bedroom. Other aspects of context include things like cultural implications, timing of the communication, relationship to other events as well as the unfolding flow of communication as it is occurring. A master of W-communication will track all these things and more as they communicate, giving them significantly more weight and attention than the average person, and in turn accessing significantly more information.

Roye was a master of W-communication as I am defining it here, and more importantly to my purposes at the time, he was a master at teaching others how to become masterful W-communicators including their self and somatic communication ... and in how to use them to create their intended outcomes on their own and with others.

"Doing the exercise" over and over, innumerable times, under Roye's direct supervision, installed a level of communication mastery in me that was beyond what I was capable of considering before we began working together ... even when I had no idea what the exercise was or what it was intended to induce. Although at the time it was beyond my comprehension, I can now recognize that Roye was using very sophisticated hypnotic protocol to teach me what he was doing, including the use of misdirection to prevent me from getting in my own way as I was learning. Instead of depending on the patterns of comfort and familiarity installed in my years of traditional, formal learning ... including all the "bad learning" that came along with that ... I was "learning how to learn" all over again, from the beginning.

Once again I realized I was in the spell of a W-communication master ... using a W-learning approach to teach me ... and the outcome was impressive ... much more than I hoped for or I knew I was getting at the time.

Chapter Notes:

[1]http://en.wikipedia.org/wiki/Solipsism
[2]http://en.wikipedia.org/wiki/Empiricism

Chapter Eight:
The Abyss

"Man has no permanent and unchangeable I.

Every thought, every mood, every desire, every sensation, says 'I'"

- G.I. Gurdjieff
In Search Of The Miraculous

CHAPTER EIGHT

Ontological Distress

When I first stepped onto the journey I had begun with Roye in Pemberton at the Blue Dell Farm Hypnotorium I was truly lost, even more so than I knew at the time. What I thought of as ontological longing was in fact out and out ontological distress ...

The sense I had back then was like vertigo ... falling endlessly from an enormous height with the ground rushing up at me, flailing helplessly, trying to stop myself from falling to no avail ... and knowing with certainty that I was about crash and burn.

The sense of helplessness was the worst part. I knew I was not just off course ... I was totally lost. I did not even know where I was headed, let alone how I could possibly get there ... if, or when, I ever figured out where I was supposed to be headed. When I mustered the courage to scratch at the surface of my discontent I came up feeling even more lost, because I had no idea who was doing the scratching. Who the "I" experiencing the scratching? With each new realization as my awareness expanded, my discomfort increased. By now I was experiencing full-blown ontological crisis ... I had crossed well beyond the threshold of mere ontological distress.

**Simply put, I had no idea who I was ...
how to find who "I" was ... or that there was any sense of solid ground where I could stand.**

I knew I could not survive "like this" ... that something had to give, and it was likely to be my sanity. Something had to be done, but I literally had no idea what to do. What I did was a combination of things, beginning with giving up completely. I walked away from my life as I knew it to be ... all of it. My career in architecture was the first sacrificial offering. When I stopped being an architect I no longer had a professional identity I could fall back upon. Financial disaster shortly followed the sacrifice of my career and professional identity. Within about a year of walking away from the professional practice of design, I was chasing money on a monthly basis just to keep the lights on and the telephone working. In addition to everything else that was going on, the edifice of my marriage was tottering and soon thereafter toppled in a ruined heap as well. I knew I was at the end of my wits when I found myself dumped on my butt, sitting on a curb laughing because I had fallen off the sidewalk trying to cross the street shortly after trying to drown my sorrows at the bottom of a bottle of Scotch whiskey on New Year's Eve.

I was never much of a drinker ... maybe a glass of wine or two with dinner. On occasion when I would go out with friends and have a drink, my drink of choice was and remains Single Malt (Scotch) Whiskey ... especially a good Single Malt. A big night out might be two drinks in four hours or so, and then home to bed. But on that first New Year's Eve without my son, because I had recently split up with my ex-wife, it all seemed to come crashing down around me, and I went for it ... straight to the bottom of the bottle. For what it is worth ... it did not help at all, although the comic relief was welcome.

My brother helped me up from my inelegant position on the curbside, and we continued our late night/early morning sobering walk-about. I began thinking about what to do ... what could I do. I did what most folks at a moment like this do ... the most familiar and comfortable thing possible. In my case that meant deciding on a course of action and learning how to succeed on it. I had already begun studying NLP and I had made a preliminary decision to become an NLP Trainer. The most logical thing in the world was to recommit and devote myself to learning like I had been taught and trained to do since I was first introduced to schooling at the age of five or so.

Fortunately for me when I met Roye he saw through my veil of delusion at first glance. Rather than letting me continue in the delusion that "education is the great leveler" or that "formal education and a degree from a good school will guarantee your success" - he stopped me cold. From that moment he began forcing me to look inward rather than outward for a way to save myself. Instead of trying to solve my problems from the outside-in he began to lead me down a different road ... one that positioned me from the inside-out.

The road Roye pointed out to me had two distinct and specific attributes that were unfamiliar to me at the time. The first and most important of the two was to begin by resetting my internal experience of Being, i.e.: who I was ... and to allow a sense of direction and focus to naturally and effortlessly emerge from that position. Where I had thought to seek a way of Being as something to do that lay outside of myself, Roye directed my attention to becoming aware of what it was like to experience myself as complete ... whole, with nothing more needed or missing. Immediately what emerged for me was a sense of what he later called, "pervasive wellbeing." As the sensation of pervasive wellbeing suffused me, I experienced a massive sense of directionality to pursue and/or sustain the sense of wholeness as the basis for all of my subsequent actions.

The second thing was noticing for things to be doing. Roye directed me to put my attention on those things that were aligned with the natural expression of my Being and which matched my innate inclinations and proclivities. Roye's way was distinctly different from how I had done things in the past. Previously my modus operandi was consistent, i.e.: I had learned to identify those things which would give me the outcomes I thought I wanted and I pursued them. Whether it was a degree from a good school ... or a good career ... or even a good wife ... my selection criteria had been driven by a sense of what was missing and what I wanted to be true of me or for me. Following that path had gotten me to where I was ... drunk and nursing a bruised buttocks.

Noticing for what was a "match and fit" for me got me to Roye and onto a different path ...
at least it did after I had decided that I had enough ...
and gave up trying to do it my way, on my own.

Admitting I needed help was probably like what Alcoholics Anonymous insists upon for newcomers ... you have to start by admitting you have a problem ... and then **YOU HAVE TO DECIDE NOT TO LET THE PROBLEM DEFINE YOU.** Roye would have gone along with AA's model with a caveat ... probably something like, **"Problems only exist in the way you perceive and think about them from the particular position you are holding ... change your position and 'poof' ... no problem!"** It was magical. From the "new position" of the Ready State I was beginning to adopt I could not perceive or think about things in a way that allowed me to access problems. Literally, it was impossible to hold the new position of the Ready State and experience a problem state simultaneously ... I had to choose one or the other. I chose the Ready State.

To do that I had to give up everything I believed I knew about the world and myself, as I had come to know about them. Essentially I had to become someone else. This was my final decent into insanity as anyone qualified to pronounce me insane would most surely have done at the time. My initial decent into insanity had begun years before when I began letting go of the familiar markers of identity I had so doggedly accumulated ... my educational achievements (despite the lack of a formal degree, I had accumulated quite a bit of education and came across to most folks I met as highly educated), my professional position, my social role and status, my intimate personal relationships ... all the things that had defined me were gone ... or going. My friends began to desert me ... I cannot blame them, I was not who they thought they knew anymore.

When you truly let go ... and begin to become someone else ... the folks you know best will not have any way of knowing you any longer. You will stop being the person they know, and it will confound, confuse and frighten them. Most folks do not have the constitution to withstand the onslaught to their sense of reality to take what you will be experiencing and stand by you ... so they will leave. You could say, "they have no choice" ... and it would be correct to say so, at least from one way of looking at things. They do have no choice but to abandon you if they want to remain fixed in the reality they have built up. You are the one who has gone away, and they are simply acknowledging that by choosing not to follow.

Crashing, Burning ... and Rebuilding

As everything around me, and within me, was going to hell I began behaving badly financially by not keeping commitments I made to others. This was an old "survival" pattern of mine. In my distorted mind I was doing what I thought I had to do to survive. The only folks I felt I could truly count on during the time I descended into insanity were my parents and my brother ... and one particular cousin I grew up with who was like an older brother to me. But, when I ran my shitty financial

CHAPTER EIGHT

survival pattern in regard to a commitment I had made to my cousin, even he wavered. Fortunately for us he was newly married and his wife stepped in and kept our relationship intact when it was most shaky. My newest cousin, his wife, intervened seeing through my actions more clearly than I could see myself. She recognized that something had to be causing me to act this badly towards him ... and of course something was going on ... I was in a profound transformational crisis, but from within it I had no way of knowing it.

I was going through the personal hell of surrendering my history and identity as I knew them to be up until that point. The small act of kindness that my cousin's wife offered me made a huge difference at the time, and created an opening for me to begin to reshape my sense of myself in relation to the world and others in it. I am sure to this day she does not really know how meaningful that small intervention was for me, but it shifted the fulcrum of how I was acting towards others and began to allow me to see myself as others saw me. From there I was able to begin making some different choices that allowed me to appear aligned in the world enough that I did not wind up forcing everyone I knew to completely reject me.

Slowly I realized that my sense of reality was shattered. I realized that what I thought was "real" was all illusion. I had projected the entirety of reality as I knew it to be, from my sense of who I was, to every object and relationship that surrounded me. There was nothing I could count on and nothing that was real. I was reeling from the impact of this realization, and falling into a massive despair. My ontological longing had progressed to ontological crisis and along with that came existential despair. Not only did I not know who I was, but I had no idea what to do about it. Nothing that I experienced was meaningful enough to care about doing it. Nothing kept me motivated or taking meaningful action, except making sure that somehow I remained connected enough to the world to be present for my young son. The one thing I hung onto was that I was a father of a two year old little boy who needed me, although I knew in my heart of hearts that too was an illusion ... but one that I had to sustain for his sake if not my own.

I crashed and burned. I lost it all, except that one thing I decided to make count ... "I was a father of a two year old little boy who needed me." ... and I used that one thing as the anchor to keep me present. While I was spinning out of control I lost contact and connection with people who had been near to the center of my life. When I was in distress I simultaneously did whatever was available to distract me from my misery, and I went into hiding in full view. I was acting like a small fox caught out in the open, frenetically looking every which way for somewhere to run, but not clever enough to stay off the street in the first place. Now, I recognize it as an old stress response pattern, showing up first and most of all in my bad financial behavior. It was a pattern that I had established long before this time in my life, turning to spending money that I did not have and was not mine as though it could somehow save me from myself.

In short order I burned my credibility with most people who had trusted me by hanging them out to dry financially or by somehow abusing their trust. When they turned away from me I was angry, because I could not see what I was doing, or why they had taken offense. On the surface I looked whole as long as you did not look too closely, and at the same time the ordinary foundations and rules which keep most of us connected to society were crumbling beneath me. It was a bad time for me and I was imposing it on those around me … "share the wealth" so to speak … as misery does indeed seem to love company.

Within a period of about two years my rejection of the illusion I had called reality and my life as I had known it to be was complete. There was nothing left. I was living in a room at my parents' home struggling to get up each morning and get on with the day. On weekends, when I had my son, it was a bit better because I could focus on him and he would pull me back from the edge I was riding … always just a few moments away from crashing and burning completely. These were tumultuous times in my life. Simultaneously I was both living the adventure and rejecting the call in every way I could while doing it, I was in hell.

**Joseph Campbell tells us, when we reject the call, crisis will never be far behind. In my case that was profoundly true …
even though I was too lost to see I was in the crisis until it became unbearable.**

In those years I seemed to be going from crisis to crisis … until I finally stopped running the old pattern of dancing on the edge of disaster and accepted my fate for what it was, curling up and giving in to it. I was lost and there was nothing I could do about it, except like Odysseus on his

CHAPTER EIGHT

journey lost on the island of Calypso, continuing to live day by day until I woke from the dream. My Odyssey led from one seemingly insurmountable challenge to another, separated by moments of ecstasy. With each step I strove for relief at any cost. Like the tragic Greek hero of the story I was living was named after, I would have given up the offer of immortality and becoming as a god to simply return safely home to my beloved son.

Over the next few years I began rebuilding a life from the ashes. One of the things I could and did count on was that each time I would return to the Hypnotorium I would reset to the Ready State ... gaining some clarity about the journey I was on ... and access the resources to continue just a bit more. As I continued to return, and to learn, I began to see a shimmer of light illuminating something beyond the life I had known and believed to be the All and Everything. There in the distance was what I strove to attain, reconnection with all that was beloved and with the beloved. I was love struck by the possibility of returning to what I recognized I had once been gifted to become. All of this was happening without any possibility of my knowing that soon thereafter I would meet the woman who would in the looming future become my wife and the mother of a child yet to be ... a boon beyond my wildest dreams.

I was finding out I was more resilient than I knew. At times I felt like the dogs that Bob and I worked with ... American Staffordshire Terriers or "Pit Bulls" as most people know them. These dogs are tenacious, once they get a hold of something, to get them to let go of it would be worst than fighting the devil himself to let go of a soul he held in hell. Not even Orpheus, despite his reputation for charming cold, hard stones to weep tears of joy or sadness with the divine and dulcet tones rising from his lyre, had such a fine tune at hand to work the magic that would have caused me to let go of what I had found.

Over three hundred years ago William Congreve spoke to the dilemma faced by the lover struck in this way, fated to suffer and remain fixed on the cause of the beloved despite themselves ...

> *Musick has Charms to sooth a savage Breast,*
> *To soften Rocks, or bend a knotted Oak.*
> *I've read, that things inanimate have mov'd,*
> *And, as with living Souls, have been inform'd,*
> *By Magick Numbers and persuasive Sound.*

What then am I? Am I more senseless grown
Than Trees, or Flint? O force of constant Woe!
'Tis not in Harmony to calm my Griefs.
Anselmo sleeps, and is at Peace; last Night
The silent Tomb receiv'd the good Old King;
He and his Sorrows now are safely lodg'd
Within its cold, but hospitable Bosom.
Why am not I at Peace?
- William Congreve, "The Mourning Bride" 1697

As in Almeria's lament I was inconsolable. Despite claims that there was such music to be had and heard, I was steadfastly unwilling and unable to let go of the bone I had gotten my teeth into ... I was not to be distracted from the Adventure I had begun ...

No amount of sweet talk or music could dissuade a pitbull from hanging onto what it had put its mind on keeping. That image ... of hanging on like a pit bull, or of Odysseus staying the course ... kept me going and going on the journey I had begun. I decided that I would never let go, or give up, regardless of what happened to me or was happening around me. In some ways my life became about hanging on and seeing things through to the end ... even though I had no idea what or where that was ... or when that might come.

The resiliency and tenaciousness I was building would serve me well over the upcoming years. There were times along the way that I would think I had reached a point where I was close to the end, where I would regain a sense of reality I could count on and trust to remain. Each time, just as I thought I was near the end of the journey, any sense of security I perceived might be at hand was wrenched away ... the discomfort was searing, akin to tearing a hardened scab off of an old wound just as it is beginning to heal. These were the worst times ... more painful and difficult than the initial realization that I had fallen off the edge of consensus reality and into the abyss of chaos had been for me.

CHAPTER EIGHT

Regaining A Sense Of Sanity

When I first realized I needed help and surrendered, it was with a sense of resolution and the glimmer of hope that I might find a way back to what was real. Each time I fell I would land harder, and the idea of a way back seemed further away than ever. In the beginning of the journey I knew that my sense of reality had been false, but I still believed there was some reality I could and would find if I just stayed the course. Each time I fell again, I was reminded that reality itself was an illusion, that there is no reality beyond Being ... only our own projections launched from within. My entire life had been built on false premises ... I had been lied to, conned and cheated. None of the promises about how my life could or would turn out if I just followed the rules ... if I learned to be good and fit in ... were true. The lies were all dependent on me buying into the consensus reality I had grown up with ... and now I finally knew that there was no reality to be had, except the totality of simply being.

What I also realized was that the reality I was projecting and believed in was not even my own. That was part of the con job ... a false sense of reality had been imposed upon me and installed into me at the deepest levels of my psyche ... and I believed it fully. Those who imposed the false reality upon me, and installed it into me, had the advantage that they did so before I had any defense prepared against what they were doing ... I trusted them fully. In their defense they also fully believed in what they were doing ... they were convinced that the projection they were living themselves was real.

> ***Whatever the Thinker thinks, the Prover will prove. And if the Thinker thinks passionately enough, the Prover will prove the thought so conclusively that you will never talk a person out of such a belief, even if it is something as remarkable as the notion that there is a gaseous vertebrate of astronomical heft ("GOD") who will spend all eternity torturing people who do not believe in his religion.***
> - Robert Anton Wilson, "Prometheus Rising" 1983

When you begin to let go of the agreements held in consensus reality ... i.e.: giving up agreeing to agree with what everyone around you claims is real ... you begin to get labeled insane. Because when you begin to challenge the foundations of what holds reality together as it is understood you become a threat to all those agree to the consensus.

"Only because there is a consensus is there a reality."

Making a statement like the one directly above can get you labeled insane in some quarters. My family and friends were well convinced that something was wrong with me, maybe very wrong. One person went so far as to label what was happening to me was diagnosable as a "walking nervous breakdown." Despite whether or not I was in fact diagnosable, one thing that those around me and I could both agree upon was that I could not be counted on to play by the rules they played by any longer.

The ordinary agreements of society began to mean less and less to me. This showed up most profoundly in the relationships I had previously considered within the frame of consensus reality, and had highly valued. The first agreement to go was treating money as valuable, in the same way others around me considered it. The idea that money represented any real value simply dissolved for me. No longer believing in money being real brought up a challenge for me. In the eyes of others who still held onto the idea of money being real, my behavior became piss poor ... but, it freed me from my old pattern of abusing money and others in regard to it. I also gave up on the idea that time was fixed, and I began to treat it with great flexibility. This worked really well for me, giving me tremendous freedom ... but, it meant that I often kept people waiting because they would insist on "keeping time" as though by tracking it the could manage, control or conserve it ... such absolute and utter nonsense confounded me to no end. People around me thought this was just another sign of how my behavior had become piss poor, or maybe how I was going insane.

Looking back now, I would have to agree, i.e.: my behavior towards others was most assuredly piss poor considered within the boundaries of the conventions they held ...
and I no longer did.

CHAPTER EIGHT

Even though I know now that things can only be judged comparatively and relatively, from a particular point of view ... within relationships what is always true is whatever the person making the judgment about "truth" believes is true. Every judgment about truth that a person makes is true for them. One of the major lessons I learned from entering the crucible of change, that went along with stepping into the journey I was on, was ... if I wanted to be in any kind of a relationship I needed to be sensitive to the rules others used to make sense of the world.

Rules formed the basis of how people organize themselves in relation to their projection of reality, and how they judge the behavior of others. Everyone has a set of rules they use ... they are aware of some of the rules they use, and unaware of many others. Despite their awareness, or lack of awareness of the rules they use, rules are the basis for reality as people know it. The rules someone uses determines how they will relate to others, and whether they will enter into a relationship with them or not. Whether or not relationships continue and deepen, or fail, depends on the rules the people in them are using.

From the point of view of another person all they can know about us are our behaviors ... to them we are our behaviors. I would say it is not actually totally true that we are only our behaviors. Yet, even if this is true, ... that we are not just our behaviors ... other than what is observable, nothing else is available to determine who other people are or to evaluate the relationships we are in with them, or for them to do the same with us. This also applies to making an assessment about whether they are even sane ... "by their behaviors you shall know them." By this definition many people would fail a sanity test. However, what most people use more than observable behavior to determine who other people are and what their relationship is with them, are their own projections about others.

Using W-communication ... beginning with an awareness of our own self-communication, including our somatic communication ... allows us to begin separating our projections from our observations. Our projections AND our observations generate somatic responses we experience as "real." When we track our internal somatic communication back to the stimuli that we are responding to we can begin to recognize what is "real" as observable sensory data that exists beyond our projections, and what is simply projection. For example, my lover may be cheating on me and planning to leave me, supported by observational sensory data I have access to, and that will create a "real" somatic response … i.e.: I will feel some way about what I observe. However, I may also project all kinds of things that are not "real" in any observable way, e.g.: that I will be alone for the rest of my life, or that my lover always planned to hurt me and the entire relationship was a set up, or that I am unlovable and this is the proof … and I will have a response to those things as well, that will feel as "real" to me as my somatic responses to what is observable. Yet, I can acknowledge that the stimuli in each case is categorically different in terms of the "real-ness" of the data that is generating my responses.

With skillfulness as W-communicators we can choose what we accept as being "real." We can distinguish between what is observable and what is not. This is a critical distinction to make as we interact with others as well. It forms the basis for recognizing when others are responding to what is "real" in terms of observable shared reality, and when they are responding to a solely self-projected reality. Making this distinction gives you the option of not falling into the "trap" of their projections with them, i.e.: beginning to experience them as though they exist in external shared reality. While some would say that sharing and experiencing the projections of others is the basis of empathy and compassion, I would gladly give that up for the ability to remain beyond the reach of those projections, i.e.: self-differentiation. Only apart from the projection can I hope to get beyond the trap of the illusions, hallucinations and delusions of "reality" … for my own sake and the sake of others whom l care about deeply and love.

Some of the most powerful projections we make about others are the ones we construct about how we feel about ourselves when we are around them. If we have decided that we feel positive about ourselves when we are around them, we typically conclude positive things about them as well. If we feel poorly about ourselves when we are around them, we conclude that there is something about them causing us to feel poorly. If we have high self-esteem, we decide that the people we feel poorly around are somehow bad for us, or maybe just bad people themselves. If we have low self-esteem, we often decide that there is something wrong with us, and that we need to prove ourselves to others. In extreme cases of low self-esteem we are most beholding to those we feel the worst to be around.

CHAPTER EIGHT

Thinking that what is true of others is a function of how we feel about ourselves when we are around them is insane. Refusing to accept the idea that others make you feel one way or another requires that you begin to reject the cause and effect paradigm that consensus reality is built around. One of the first steps I began to take towards regaining my sanity was refusing to accept that others could make me feel a certain way without my consent. However, as soon as I began to accept that others could not make me feel a certain way, it meant that the inverse was also true ... I could not make them feel a certain way.

Accepting that others could not make me feel a certain way, or conversely that I could not make them feel a certain way, gave me an enormous freedom in my relationships with others, ... but from their point of view it only increased their opinion that my hold on sanity was slipping, or maybe that it had already completely slipped away.

The idea ...
"What others do is always about them and never about us."
... is extremely empowering.

To benefit as fully as possible from holding the belief, "what others do is always about them and not about us" it needs to be integrated into the way it manifests as behavior. Understanding that others are operating within boundaries defined by the rules they are using, both those they are aware of and those they are not, allows you to incorporate the full understanding that what others do is always about them and not about you. Even when someone notices something that is true about you, from your own point of view, what they noticed tells you something about what they are noticing for ... and in that way it is more about them than it is about you.

For example, according to some standards I have been overweight for much of my adult life. Other than the impact on some clothing I might like to have worn at various times it has not otherwise impacted my life. I have been and remain healthy, vital and full of energy. I have robust and satisfying relationships with others. I am satisfied in my work ... and so on. BUT ... according to the folks to whom it matters, what they notice first or most of all is that I am overweight. They do not notice a thousand and one other things that are true of me, they notice that I am overweight. That tells me as much about them as it ever could about the obvious observation they are making about me. Same thing would be true if they notice that according to their standing I might have a big nose, I am balding or have dark skin, that I am five feet ten inches tall, or that I am wearing a red shirt ... what they are noticing for is all about them, even though what they notice might be "real" as far as their observation goes.

As I began to integrate this understanding, and act in relation to it, my relationships began to shift in profound ways. I was able to put aside many of my "piss poor" behaviors and begin treating others as they wanted to be treated. When I began treating people in the way they wanted to be treated, according to their rules, people who knew me forever began to treat me as though I was finally regaining my sanity ... and people who just met me thought I must be one of the sanest people they had ever met.

Noticing for the rules people hold and use to construct their projections of reality, became one of my earliest and best "tricks" as I progressed through the first phases of my journey. I also discovered that it was one of the deepest foundational premises of W-communication as well. Being able to notice the explicit and implicit rules that govern behavior opens up the possibility of responding to the behavior within the confines of the rules being used ... and, the alternative of choosing to rewrite the rules that construct the game being played.

One of my rules has become, "He/She who writes the rules wins." ... and I believe that is true even when by winning the game they are playing they may lose themselves.

Slowly ... I began climbing out of the Abyss.

Chapter Nine:

Going Beyond the Story

"If the present world go astray, the cause is in you, in you it is to be sought."
- Dante Alighieri
The Divine Comedy

CHAPTER NINE

Freezing (Your Ass Off) In Hell

Everyone experiencing a personal transformation experiences a portion of their journey where they transit through a personal hell and must surrender to the process by looking deeply into themselves. The transformational journey demands a commitment to ruthless honesty ... at least to one's self. Many questions arise as you approach the journey and cross the threshold, two of them might be "What will the transit through hell be like?" and "How does one prepare one's self to survive the hell they will confront?"

The idea of transiting through a personal hell, like Jonah's time in the belly of the whale, has been explored artistically in many ways. Two recent cinematographic examples include George Lucas' "Star Wars" trilogy and the Wachowski brothers "Matrix" trilogy.

In the Star Wars films, the hero, Luke Skywalker, while training with Yoda, a Jedi Master, confronts himself in an underground cave on the planet Dagobah. Later on another character, Hans Solo, winds up frozen in carbonite and held by the villain Jabba the Hutt. In both of these scenes from the story we are offered examples of what it is to be in the belly of the whale.

In The Matrix trilogy the Wachowski brothers have Neo leave the relative comfort, familiarity and security of the illusion that is the Matrix and enter into the what could be called the "belly of the real world" ... leading up to the supreme ordeal of losing his eyes, then his love ... and finally his life.

There are also many other examples of the hero's journey into the belly of the whale and surviving hell in literature, for example in the masterful writing of J.R. Tolkien as he depicted it in "The Hobbit" when Bilbo Baggins descends into Golum's cave or when he enters Smaug's lair, or when Bilbo's nephew, Frodo, enters Shelob's lair in the book "Two Towers" of the Lord of the Rings series.

In in the epic poem, the Odyssey, of the journey of Odysseus and his crew back to Ithica after the siege of Troy - beginning with Poseidon's rage, the capture of the entire crew and their time in the cave of the Cyclops before blinding him and escaping ... and before sharing with us how Odysseus alone survives and returns home as told by the Greek poet Homer - is yet another example of the classic hero's tale, entering the belly of the whale, surviving hell and returning home.

The common thread in each of these tales is the theme of the hero losing their life as they knew it to be before stepping across the "Threshold of Adventure" as Joseph Campbell described it in his seminal work, "The Hero With a Thousand Faces." At the very least the hero must descend and sacrifice themselves in a figurative hell, often of their own making, before returning redeemed and ready to reclaim their life.

One of the earliest Western classics documenting the transformational journey is Alighieri's 14th Century epic poem the "Divine Comedy" - also written as a trilogy. Alighieri begins the trilogy with "Inferno" ... the Italian word for hell. In the "Inferno" Dante leads his readers through Hell's nine circles.

All of Dante's circles of hell are located within the Earth at progressively deeper levels, with progressively worsening descriptions of the sins and torments suffered by the souls caught in each. Every circle is reserved for those who have a committed a specific sin:

- **First Circle (Limbo)**
- **Second Circle (Lust)**
- **Third Circle (Gluttony)**
- **Fourth Circle (Greed)**
- **Fifth Circle (Anger)**
- **Sixth Circle (Heresy)**
- **Seventh Circle (Violence)**
- **Eighth Circle (Fraud)**
- **Ninth Circle (Treachery)**

The First Circle is applied to folks where the sins they have committed are unintended, as well as for those who had never accepted Christ. It is quite lush as Dante presents it to us, the a final resting place for virtuous, but "unsaved" pagans and the unbaptized. Not a bad place to wind up for eternity ... and should you find yourself there you would be in good company, including many famous Greeks and Romans, e.g.: Homer, Plato, Julius Cesar, and a number of mythological folks as well, like Hector and Orpheus.

CHAPTER NINE

From there you begin to spiral down to the lower reserved circles for those who have deliberately sinned. The first level of punishment in hell for those who have sinned is found at the second circle. Here we find the lustful. These folks have been led astray by their uncontrolled appetites and are buffeted by unending winds and violent storms. The suffering they bear is akin to the way they lived their lives, constantly pulled and pushed about by their desires.

At each circle the sins and the punishments increase in intensity. The first four circles of sin, from level two through five are for the sins of weakness shared by those who lack the ability to control themselves in some way. These are the least condemned or punished sins. At the sixth circle it begins to get interesting in a new way as the sins at this level and below are intentional, and sins of intention are treated far more harshly than those of uncontrolled or uncontrollable passions.

In sixth circle Dante meets the heretics. Heresy is a sin of thinking, and committing it requires both awareness and intention. It is the belief that mortals have no soul, or if they do it dies with their body. For this they are forever condemned to be consumed in tombs of flames, never again to perceive a future because they themselves have denied the future of the soul.

Below the sixth circle of hell, as the decent into the deeper, darker reaches progresses, the punishments become significantly worst and there are levels within levels to consider. Hell from the seventh circle downwards is reserved for violent and malicious sinners. The seventh circle has within it three circles, each progressively housing more offensive sinners. While the seventh circle is reserved for violent sinners, i.e.: those who violently sin against others and G-d, the last two circles are reserved for the most offensive sins of all "fraud" and "treachery" … considered even more abhorrent than direct and open violence by Dante.

In the eighth circle of hell there are ten "bolgie" (Italian: ditches of stone). Each "bolgia" ("bolgie" singular) represents unique and different kinds of frauds, deceivers of others who sin by virtue of their deceptions, each with their own unique torments applied to them. Flatterers are covered in human excrement representing the words they spoke. Corrupt politicians are covered in boiling pitch representing their sticky fingers as they engaged in dealing under the table. Dante devotes an entire bolgia to evil counselors and advisors who did not engage in corruption themselves except for the advice and direction they gave to others; these folks are wrapped in flames, forever consuming them and preventing them from connecting with any other being for eternity.

The ninth and final circle of hell according to Dante is reserved exclusively for traitors, and in this circle there are four rounds. The sinners condemned to the ninth circle are distinct from those in the eighth circle in that they betrayed a relationship they were in with another. In Dante's cosmology this is the most grievous sin of all, to betray someone personally. Each of the rounds in the ninth circle holds ever more egregious betrayers according to Dante. At the very center surrounded by the foulest mortal betrayers in history, Brutus and Cassius the betrayers of Julius Cesar and Judas the betrayer of Christ, is Satan - who in betraying G-d became the greatest betrayer on earth or in heaven.

Dante's construction of the cosmology of circles of hell has always intrigued me. In that cosmology Dante presents us with the idea that, "sins against one's self are less contemptible than those against others." From another point of view Dante's cosmology of hell suggests that, "sins of the mind" are worst than "sins of the body." However, Dante makes it clear that at the very center of hell we find the worst sin of all, the sin of treachery … betrayal. I agree with Dante about betrayal, I do so for different reasons than the one he seems to propose.

I believe that the sin of betrayal leads us to experience our own unique form of personal hell.

In the "Inferno" the punishment for betrayal is being forever frozen in ice. The worse the betrayal, the worse the position in which the sinner is frozen. Those closest to Satan are frozen forever in contorted positions from which they find no relief, and the three most abominable sinners according to Dante are eternally chewed on by one of Satan's three faces.

Dante's description of the torment of the eight and ninth circle of hell also fits metaphorically with the punishments we inflict upon ourselves for self-deception and self-betrayal. Each deceiver in the eighth circle has their own unique torment relating to the way they have deceived others. From my experience of working with others and my own experience this fits the punishment we incur when we deceive ourselves. We become trapped by the lies we tell ourselves, exactly prescribing the way those lies limit us uniquely … e.g.: if we flatter ourselves we become trapped by self flattery, if we make predictions about our future based on historical evidence we are condemned to live within the boundaries of our history, etc. Reading about the eight circle of hell in Dante's "Inferno" portrays the multitude of ways we deceive ourselves and the kinds of punishment we can expect to inflict upon ourselves when we do. Yet, it is only when we get to the ninth circle of hell in Dante's cosmology, as he laid it out in the "Inferno," that we begin to see the true suffering we inflict upon ourselves. The sin I refer to here is self-betrayal, and our punishment is becoming frozen in our suffering without relief.

Separation From Self

Akin to the sins of the ninth circle of hell as Dante depicts them in the first book of his classic trilogy, the "Divine Comedy" ... "Inferno" ("Hell") ... the sin we inflict upon ourselves resides in how we betray the personal relationship we have with ourselves, i.e.: when we deny who we are ... we commit the unpardonable sin of ontological denial. When we deny ourselves ontologically, betraying ourselves in the most essential way conceivable, we suffer the fate of becoming frozen in the position we adopt. We become trapped ... accepting as true that we are the false persona we project.

Despite the fact that we are trapped by an illusion, we have no choice but to hold the illusion and the projections that emanate from it as "real." Since we are frozen by the belief that the illusion we hold regarding ourselves is real, it follows that we experience everything within that position as being real as well. This was the hell I realized I had descended into. My realization that I was in hell drove me to begin the transformational quest I had already begun when I first met Roye. Like the souls writhing in hell, up to that point I had tried to free myself from my self-imposed, distorted, frozen position without success. As I became more aware of the illusion I was living the suffering only continued and increased. The ability to realize how we suffer as a result of our choices and the actions we take is a remarkable thing unto itself.

As long as I was willing to accept the illusion I was living as real, I experienced little to no suffering within it. Accepting the illusion I was in as the only possibility, I remained capable of experiencing something akin to ecstasy ... i.e.: I experienced ecstasy as long as I was succeeding within the illusion I was living within. Suffering only came to me when I failed to succeed within the framework of the illusion as I knew it. This suffering was easily relieved by redoubling my efforts within the illusion, and doing what it took to succeed as defined within it. One of the "powers" that the illusion possesses is the "power" to reward those who continue to accept it as being real. Of course the rewards are only "real" within the context of the illusion, meaning that they too are just illusions.

A personal challenge of mine was the confusion that my suffering was existential when it was actually ontological. For years I pursued relief from my suffering by trying to figure out what to be doing, and then diligently following through when I thought I discovered what it was that I was meant to be doing. Regardless of the number of times I followed this pattern I continued to experience the essential suffering of my soul that was beyond the reach of any existential or pragmatic remedy. Despite some sense of relief at times, no amount of "doing" was sufficient to relieve my essential distress.

Another challenge was overcoming the illusion of "reward" that also seemed to pose some relief. I could delude myself into believing that if I could get the "right stuff" I would be okay. The "right stuff" might be anything ... from getting my driver's license to being in a relationship with a girl I was interested in dating. Later on the "right stuff" became "bigger stuff" ... like a particular car I wanted to own and drive, or a house I wanted to live in ... or getting married to a woman I was in love with ... at other times the "right stuff" might be the career or business I wanted to be in, begin or own, or it could be the whole "lifestyle" shebang I wanted to be living at the time. During this phase, I became rather good at getting stuff when I put my mind to it, despite the cost of doing so - to myself or others.

While I thought that I just had not picked the right thing to be doing, or the right stuff to get, after years of running on the treadmill of this illusion I finally had to admit that in spite of all my motion I was not getting anywhere. I needed a new plan of action ... or so I thought. As long as I was trapped by the illusion that something I could do would lead me to satisfaction, I was incapable of considering that nothing I could do would satisfy the yearning I was experiencing.

CHAPTER NINE

I was in Dante's ninth circle of hell ... frozen by my own projections and suffering at their hand.

I believed I had no choice in this matter, I thought the persona that had been built up for me, around me and that I ultimately stepped into willingly and wore as my own, was "me" - not a mask I was wearing. Along with the sin of self-betrayal I added the sin of self-deception. I began to tell myself the stories I needed to recite that would sustain the illusion I was now living. At one point I had been in touch with something essential within me. I was free to experience the world beyond illusion for what it was ... and when I did my world was complete and there was no suffering. When I was living within that story the world was whole and I was simply present to the wholeness of the world, there was no separation between the two ... me, and the world as I experienced it.

In order to sustain an experience of ourselves as separate from the world, we need a story of separation. As soon as we are introduced to such a story, and adopt it as our own, we begin to experience suffering. The foundation of the separation story is built on the idea that we somehow exist distinctly apart from everything we experience. This essential, key component of the separation story forms the basis of the way we begin to consider how we want things to be other than how they are ... i.e.: the first of the sins in Dante's cosmology of hell, lust ... desire. This is the same sin that virtually every other system of wisdom points to as well, e.g.: in Buddhism Siddhartha Gautama recognizes desire, along with the ignorance of desire and its release, as the cause of all suffering.

- If we follow the path of wisdom, in order to relieve our suffering, we must let go of desire.

- I discovered that in order to let go of desire I first had to let go of the separation story I had come to believe represented what was real.

However, giving up the story is easier said than done. I first came across the idea of alternative realities in some of the books I was reading, like Robert Anton Wilson's "Prometheus Rising" and his description in that book of "reality tunnels." Many of those books told different stories than the one I knew. I was reading these books and learning about alternative stories from around the age of eleven. The idea that my "reality" was not "real" (i.e.: the exclusive true and correct story of reality) shook me up and created a compulsion to find out more, but it was still not enough for me to give up the story I was living.

In the years between the ages of eleven and fifteen I explored a bunch of stories that were different from my own. A large number of the alternative stories I was exploring came out of the Oriental tradition, as my interest in martial arts led to many stories with an Eastern or Oriental flavor to them. I came across one story in particular, which caught my attention, and has held it for the last thirty-eight years, "The Judoka" by W.D. Norwood. The main character in that story lives outside of the ordinary rules that society plays by for the most part. He lived on a beach sleeping under the stars, not on a bed in a house. He hunted for his food, instead of buying it in a store. In some other ways he was quite "normal" … he fell in love with a girl, fought with 'bad' guys … but basically he lived life on his own terms. The story appealed to me in ways I could not begin to explain.

Norwood's story, and the main character he created, presented a possibility of how life could be if I were to let go of what I knew to be my "personal identity" as it had been shaped and formed within the story I had been living within up to that point in my life. My personal identity was the sum total of all I had come to believe and value, e.g.: go to school, get good grades, get a good job, find a girl, get married, buy a house, have children, raise your children, retire … and die. There were many aspects to this story all falling in line with the idea that I should "be good and fit in" … like being honest, hard working, responsible, respectable … and living up to these expectations meant I might have the reward of dying happy. Norwood was somehow able to convey the fundamental idea to me that all of this however was a story … not "real" … just a story. From the understanding that I was living inside of a story … a story that I was scripting as I lived it … I began to understand I could script a different story for myself.

I was absorbing the structure of mythic form as I read about many different kinds of characters in many different kinds of stories. The idea that stories had the potential to transform held sway over me for many years across the reading I continued doing. In the years that followed I found I could also find stories that were told in other ways too,

CHAPTER NINE

like in the many films I had watched and began watching in a new way ... with my eyes (and ears, heart and soul) much more widely opened.

When I encountered the writing of Joseph Campbell the structure I had absorbed implicitly became explicit. Instead of simply being drawn to the characters in stories that appealed to me, I started choosing characters and stories for what they could teach me about regaining access to my core self. I searched for characters that would illustrate and illuminate the possibility of reshaping my life to match and fit who I was essentially. Meeting Roye in the Hypnotorium at the Blue Dell Farm in Pemberton brought it all together for me into a package that allowed me to get at what I had been searching for, albeit unbeknownst to me then.

Roye tapped into the mythic structure I had been ingesting and assimilating using the methodology of W-learning, and helped me to express what remained hidden in plain sight. By creating the friction I needed, Roye allowed me to see myself through my interactions with him and in the interactions I had with others in his presence, while under his guidance and direction. Over time as our many levels of relationship deepened ... as teacher/student, mentor/mentee, master/apprentice ... he extended his input and influence to what I shared with him about my life and the work I was doing that did not occur in his presence.

As Roye guided me on my Journey he added in new learning as well, things that went beyond what I had considered before meeting him ... about what it is to become fully human, and to arrive at becoming fully myself. The great gift I already had when I first arrived at the Hypnotorium and met Roye was the gift of W-learning ... the great gift or boon, the one that Joseph Campbell points to in the Hero's Journey that comes about as a result of making it through the trials and tribulations we face when we undertake our Adventure, was mastery in the art and science of W-communication. Beginning with the powerful insights that came from mastering self-communication, including the subtle and sublime information that became available to me by learning to attend to my somatic communication, I could finally begin the fundamental reshaping of my life "from the inside out" that was the point all along ... I began to reclaim my wholeness.

Mastering W-communication opened me to receive all the other gifts and boons Joseph Campbell describes come to the Hero who take on the Adventure and complete the Journey as well ...

- **Father Atonement** (resolution of parental/family/generational issues)
- **Sacred Marriage** (finding and experiencing true love, compassion, commitment, fidelity …)
- **The Elixir** (abundant vitality and health, both physical and mental)
- **The Totem** (knowledge of my true being and calling)

Once I began to truly know myself, releasing the image and illusion of the persona and mask I was wearing happened without effort. Unbeknownst to me I was again discovering myself, who I am, simply by having the experience of my life … **I was becoming ready to Return.**

Distinctions Of Distress

A few years after I started developing the MythoSelf Process model in the 1990s, I had already begun to think about the idea of "mythological distress." When I made the initial decision about radically changing my life, that led to my walking away from my practice as an architect, the dissolution of my marriage, and the rest of the ruin that followed, I did not understand what I was getting myself into. I did understand, or at least I had a sense, that the story I was living was no longer big enough to contain me. I needed a new story … probably a bigger story, definitely a better story … than the one I had. I did not know it at the time, but it was inevitable that I would begin looking for that new story. I had crossed over the boundary of mythological distress, i.e.: living within a story that was not a match and fit for who I truly was … with a hopeful eye towards the possibility of mythological resolution.

When I first encountered NLP in the late 1980s I thought I would be learning an alternative way to deal with psychological distress. Partly what attracted me to NLP, was that I thought I would gain another piece of the puzzle that would help me to make sense of the world, and in so doing relieve my distress. In the early 1990s, as my life was disintegrating, some folks I knew thought it might be a good idea for me to seek traditional psychological help. NLP seemed like a fast track, solution oriented approach to dealing with problems often addressed using psychological interventions. Now I believe it would be more accurate to think of NLP as a powerful model of communication performance strategies that can (and often does) make a significant difference in someone's quality of thinking ... especially in their decision-making strategy. In my opinion NLP is the most direct and useful technology available to rectify cognitive ill-formedness ... or the habit of poorly organized thinking, as it is expressed and held in the ways we communicate, both to ourselves and with others.

To my way of thinking "applied epistemology" would be a good meta-description of NLP . As an applied epistemological approach ... addressing "how we know what we know" ... NLP can resolve what are often thought of as psychological issues that are in reality issues of cognitive ill-formedness. When the issues at hand are really manifestations of poorly organized ways of thinking and/or communicating, i.e.: cognitive ill-formedness, I would go as far as to say the NLP may well be the best intervention ... and this is especially true when the issues we are dealing with are linguistically ill-formed.

I do not mean to imply that no issues are psychological or physiological in origin (including issues of neuro-chemical imbalance). Of the varying kinds of distress we experience as part of the human condition ... psychological distress, physiological distress, existential distress, epistemological distress, ontological distress, mythological distress, etc. ... here is the distinction I would apply as unique to **Psychological Distress: "A condition of the mind that interferes with, or makes impossible, a high quality of perception, cognition, decision-making and/or behavioral response, that may be organic in nature."** I do not claim any official, formal or recognized capacity to form such a definition, but I do suggest it is nonetheless a very useful distinction to apply in "**keeping separate things separate**" - another distinction I highly value.

I use a similar distinction for epistemological distress. Here is the distinction I apply to **Epistemological Distress: "When what we believe we know to be true is incorrect, distorted or so poorly organized that it makes it difficult or impossible for us to make high-quality decisions or take action using appropriately aligned behavior to produce the outcomes we intend."**

In my case a psychological or epistemological intervention, NLP based or otherwise, could never resolve what was ailing me. My distress was ontological, a "disorder" of being, not thinking. Here's what I have to say about, **Ontological Distress: "The recognition that you are not having the experience of your life, and cannot bring the system to rest because you are sustaining a false identity that has been imposed upon and accepted by you."** The ontological distress I was experiencing was contained and sustained by the story I was living, creating mythological distress.

> **Mythological Distress: When the story that we are relating to, operating from and living out of ... as we hold it semantically and somatically ... is not our own and does not represent us ontologically as we know ourselves to be, it prevents us from perceiving ourselves or the world-at-large as we know them in a way that inherently matches our experience ... and the story interferes with our sense-making, as well as our ability to make high-quality decisions and take action that fits the outcomes we intend to create..**

While in mythological distress we are trapped by a story that is not our own, and are living within the limits the story imposes on us.

All of this and more was true of me ... therefore I needed a new story.

Ultimately, the greatest challenge of mythological distress is in how it prevents us from becoming fully human ... fully ourselves ... i.e.: of finding and living your own story and having the experience of your life.

One of the advantages of the NLP model as a potent communication performance technology was that it gave me some new tools to begin working with stories. However, my ability to re-form my story and the stories of others that I had begun working with became extraordinary when I began to get the distinctions of W-communication under my belt ... far beyond what had been possible within the limits of the NLP model as I had learned and knew them. The distinction of working with what I am calling "mythological distress" as I've delineated it was a new distinction as far as I could tell. While NLP works extensively with metaphor, working with mythic form is not something I know of that any one practicing NLP was, or is, talking about or doing. I had come across people in the NLP community and elsewhere who sometimes called themselves "applied mythologists" working with myths, i.e.: using storytelling as a way of helping others. Hearing specific kinds of stories, e.g.: myths, folk tales, folklore and wisdom stories from various cultures and traditions that have been vetted through the ages - people can and do come to new insights and revelations about themselves and the world around them. In this way storytelling can be powerful and have a significant impact on the people who experience it.

"Storytelling" per say, or incorporating the use of "ritual" and "tradition" as some applied mythologists do in their work, does not address mythological distress specifically by using W-learning and W-communication methodically.

Some folks I had been learning from incorporated working with stories in a completely different way than by storytelling as many people think about it as retelling the great myths, folk and fairy tales, or the traditional stories gathered from people who developed them over centuries or possibly even millennia. In the NLP community telling "stories" as a part of hypnotic communication protocol is common. These stories are used metaphorically and NLPers follow along in the tradition of folks like the great medical hypnotherapist, Milton H. Erickson, MD. when using them. Sometimes these kinds of metaphors are referred to as "teaching tales" ... i.e.: a story told with an intention to convey an idea or teach a lesson embedded within the story. This technique, i.e.: using therapeutic metaphor, is more direct and may have a more powerful impact for generating change than storytelling in general. I have personally seen the application of therapeutic metaphors work magic in the lives of people when used by a gifted practitioner.

As powerful as the use of storytelling and therapeutic metaphor might be, neither of them directly speaks to, or addresses, mythological distress.

Distinguishing between myth and mythic form is one of the critical aspects of understanding what I mean by mythological distress. Myths are the stories themselves, whether we use this word to refer to revered traditional tales drawn from a given culture, or more loosely to refer to a story that is told mythologically. What I am calling mythic form refers to addressing the deep structural form of the stories people use to create, describe and project personal and social realities, i.e.: how the stories are built, not what they are built from or what they are about.

Maybe the most significant story we tell is our autobiographical narrative - our "Life Story" - the story that defines a person first to themselves, and only secondarily to others. Our Life Story is always organized mythologically ... yet it is not a myth in the ordinary sense of a story to be told, heard or read. Much of the autobiographical narrative is never expressed or explicitly experienced consciously, even by the person who creates it. This story is only partially contained in the kind of abstractions, symbols or language that are accessible in ordinary thinking form. The rest of the magnificent story of your life resides in somatic form outside of the conscious access available to most people. Yet, despite the implicit nature of the story, the owner of the autobiographical narrative lives in relation to it and it informs them about every detail of their being themselves. Reality as we know it literally emerges from and rests upon this story, and yet most people know only a small part of it as it exists for them.

A greater challenge than not knowing your Life Story is when it does not fit who you are, what you want to make manifest and how you intend to bring that into being in your life. You can survive and prosper without ever knowing your autobiographical narrative explicitly, but when it does not fit you will be in virtually constant distress ... suffering and striving with little relief or satisfaction. The most common issue people have with their autobiographical narrative is that they often outgrow it early on and never bother updating it.

When we have outgrown the essential Life Story that defines us and our reality it becomes a straight-jacket limiting our every thought and action. This is the experience of mythological distress.

We can never become who we are destined to be, or manifest anything near the totality of our potential, until we update our Life Story to fit who we are today ... semantically in our thoughts and words and somatically in our bodies and actions ... with enough room built in to accommodate who we are capable of becoming.

As I started becoming aware of the impact my Life Story had on the quality of my life, I made becoming masterful in working with my Life Story central to my quest. As I worked on and inside of my Life Story, I developed the kind of mastery necessary to help others reveal, identify and work with theirs as well.

Mastery in working on and with the deep mythic form* that resides in and guides us ... i.e.: the essential structure of the Life Story we must discover, design and take charge of to become ourselves ... is the ultimate destination.

*NOTE: In honor of the significance of working with mythic form, as well as in homage to those I follow, I called the work I do the MythoSelf Process.

Chapter Ten:

Owning Your Adventure

"Sensation Is Its Own Phenomena"
- Laura McFarland, N.D.

CHAPTER TEN

The Story Of Your Life

"Learning your Life Story leads you to LEARNING WHO YOU ARE ... NOT ABOUT WHO YOU ARE ...
but the actuality of being and remaining present to the experience of who you are in every moment."
- Joseph Riggio, Ph.D

For some people the statement above may be the most controversial statement in this book, at least for any or the more philosophically inclined folks out there. However, without question, the leading statement of this chapter is surely the most paradoxical one in the book so far.

Clearly your Life Story is NOT who you are. Your Life Story, or any story is just that ... a story. This particular story, your Life Story, happens to be about YOUR life ... in that way it is uniquely significant to you and for you.

All stories are constructs, a representation, an abstraction ... all the things I have been arguing against from the beginning of this book. To keep the record straight I am NOT saying that your Life Story IS WHO ARE, i.e.: YOUR BEING. I am saying that knowing your Life Story intimately will lead you to discovering who you are, as well as who you are becoming, i.e.: the ontological form that is YOUR BEING. Yet, YOUR BEING is not and will never be a story ... nor will any story ever contain it ... not even your own Life Story.

Before I go further I want to let you know that I think this chapter holds the key to how to free yourself of distress and begin having the life you desire ... it contains what I think of as the secret to becoming free to have the experience of your life. I want to take a moment here and implore you to stick with it through what may seem like dense, unfamiliar and even uncomfortable material.

I'm being explicit about this because I recognize that it may feel like the paragraphs above go around in circles, crazily looping back onto themselves in every sentence. I get that if you were to read and re-read these paragraphs again, rather than gaining clarity, they might just seem to become denser, further obfuscating the message. However, this not my intention, it is a trick that was foisted on you long before I came along and wrote this book. It is a trick imposed upon you in what I call "bad learning." I would argue that it is bad learning that creates virtually all the insanity we see around us in society, except for some of it that is purely neurological in nature. I even think getting past bad learning might make a substantial difference in the lives of the people afflicted by neurological issues that we have come to label "insane" in our insane world.

Let me go further and say that most people have been taught they are not able to deal with "dense" subject matter, like understanding themselves and the complex world around them They have learned that what seems complex is best left to geniuses and experts, who they have also been taught they clearly are not. As a result of this foolish message, rather than seeking to become a "wise fool" … or as I prefer to think of those people who take up the challenge, accept the call to adventure and begin the journey of becoming fully human and in the process fully themselves, "Apprentices of Wonder" … most folks simply learn to shun any intellectual material, starting with big words.

For instance most folks are never taught the fundamental distinctions between ontology and epistemology, or the distinctions between "what is true or real" and "how we know what we know to be true or real." We have been taught that "what we know" is "what is true and real" … in other words our thoughts and experience about reality are truly reality. I have been doing all that I can to build the argument that nothing could be further from the truth or real. In fact I have been arguing that we can never get to the truth of reality, because we are innately limited to having only our own experience of what is "true or real."

Now, I am afraid you may feel like you are even further from clarity than before, but I promise if you stay the course it will indeed become clear to you.

Despite how the information in the few paragraphs above may seem to be spinning around itself and going nowhere, I can assure you we are nearer to the point of this whole storybook than at any other moment within it.

The information about the distinction between ontology and epistemology is critical to making sense of the paragraphs in question above, and to making sense of your own life too. It was a cornerstone that I needed to acquire and securely set before I could move from the insanity of my life to becoming sane. So, before I leap forward lets linger here for a bit longer, on the distinction between ontology and epistemology, and I will clear up any confusion so we can go forth freely on common ground ... towards the light of sanity together.

Ontology simply refers to "what is" ... the extant, manifest beingness of things or ideas. If we want to simplify further we might say, **"Ontology refers to what exists."** While this statement may seem straightforward enough, the human condition makes it very hard to know what actually exists beyond ourselves. Some philosophers argue even knowing that we ourselves exist is in and of itself a conundrum ... the one that Rene Descartes tried to clear up when he stated "Cognito Ergo Sum." ... "I think, therefore I am."

Epistemology refers to how we know what we know, and according to some the pursuit of how we know what we know to be true, and therefore real. The conundrum of epistemology comes along with Descartes supposedly ontological solution. He must have believed something like, "What I think I know to be true and real must exist, and I know that I think, therefore I am real."

If Descartes did not believe that his thinking was truly real he could not have arrived at the conclusion that he was truly real. Yet how could Descartes know with certainty that he was not the artifact of someone's imagination projected into a character that thinks about himself, as in an animated film. Only in believing that their thinking is their own could someone possibly know that they were not just a mental artifact of someone else's thinking. As I read it, therefore, Descartes' conclusion that he exists because he thinks must be an epistemological conclusion, and does not speak ontologically to what must be extant and manifest in a world that exists beyond Descartes own thoughts.

"Epistemology is the study of the mental artifacts of ontology, i.e.: constructs, representations, abstractions, symbols and language representing what is true or real, that allow us to know about, explore and manipulate our experience of what is true or real."
- Joseph Riggio, Ph.D.

However, more to the point, we only know about what is true or real based on the mental artifacts that we use to interact with truth and reality as we experience them, and the primary mental artifact we have access to are the stories we create. The core of "epistemological truth and reality" then must be the stories we create that contain the mental artifacts we use to experience, know about and interact with what we perceive to be true or real, i.e.: what we hold to be extant and manifest beyond ourselves … ontological truth or reality.

Within the total construction of reality as we experience, know about and interact with it resides a unique construction we know about as ourselves, i.e.: who we are … our ontological form. What we know about our ontological form, and the way we know about it, is contained in the story we use to represent ourselves to ourselves and others, our autobiographical narrative or Life Story. Even if we ourselves do not exist, i.e.: that we are simply a conscious projection or mental artifact of some truly real, extant and manifest being, the story we have access to about us must exist. In this way our Life Story transcends the epistemological conundrum and crosses the ontological gap, i.e.: our story is the most truly real thing we have access to or possess.

Based on our Life Story we also manifest behavioral responses that are aligned with, and fit into, the way that story is constructed. Others know us based on our behaviors, which are externalized reflections and manifestations of our Life Story. If we want to experience ourselves and reality differently, or if we want others to experience and know us differently, the key to shifting is to make the changes that we desire in the way they are contained in our Life Story.

If/when you change your Life Story your reality changes, and the reality of who you are to and for others changes as well …
<u>Change your Life Story</u> … and you <u>Change Your Life</u>.

One of the most important things you need to know about stories now is that a story is just that, a story. Your Life Story is just a tale about who you have been, who you or others think you are, and possibly where you or others believe you are aimed and going. As a story the bits and pieces that comprise it are always selective, they are never the whole thing itself, i.e.: the unabridged representation of totality of an experience.

Your Life Story points to who you are, it is NOT who you are. There is however a subtle dynamic constantly in play between who you are and the story of your life ... as they inform one another they continuously reshape who you know yourself to have been and know yourself to be, and therefore how you aim yourself in regard to who you are becoming. When you get how this works you put your Life Story in the service of YOUR BEING. This leads us to what may be the biggest, most significant question you can ask about your Life Story ... WHO is (the one) telling the tale - and - WHO is (the one) hearing it???

"Who We Are ..."

As a part of everyone's Life Story there will be a chapter entitled, "Who We Are," all about "your" people the ones you are attached to by blood and history. In some cultures and families attach deep and lasting implication to the "Who We Are" storyline. This part of your Life Story, "Who We Are," was being crafted for you by others long before you were born.

I have been with Jewish families who place great importance on their identity as Jews ... their collective history, often the contradictions of persecution and privilege (i.e.: as the "Chosen Ones") represent a great deal of how they now think of themselves and the values they hold as sacred. I've been with Chinese families who place great emphasis on "the family" ... and how relationships and the obligations they entail have shaped and continue to shape their lives. I grew up in a traditional Italian-American family with its own stories and the implications of those stories on the individuals within the immediate and extended family of which I am a part. I could share similar tales about Danish families I know well, or of my American friends or the families of mixed religious, ethnic and racial backgrounds I know well ... Swedish and Indonesian, Italian and Moroccan ... the list could go on and on. Each family, and each person within it, has their story.

There are other stories about "Who We Are" as well, some that are a given by virtue of context and some that are chosen. Almost all nations have a story about "Who We Are" ... and some degree of nationalism exists in virtually everyone I have ever met, even those who have grown up in multiple nations as multi-nationals. There are stories about the schools we attended, the organizations we belong to and the church, temple or mosque we attend where we worship. Some of the groups we belong to we have chosen ourselves, e.g.: fraternal or sororal societies, civic organizations, or non-profit groups, we chose to associate with and support. Some of the groups we belong to are chosen for us, like the religion we are born into or the nation of our birth.

Some of the groups we have belonged to were a function of the environment we grew up in … a given so to speak, e.g.: our early schooling experiences are most often a function of where we lived when we began attending school as children, or the neighborhood friends we had growing up. As we mature we may choose to continue to identify and associate with these early affiliations … or we may choose to move on and away from them. In either case their influence in our lives is part of the Life Story we carry forth. The events and experiences of our past often continue to shape us, influencing our sense of identity before and beyond our conscious awareness.

Among the most influential stories we hold are about the groups we believe we have chosen to become members of ourselves, both formal and informal groups. Most adults have belonged to informal groups comprised of friends that have shifted and changed as they matured. Some of these friendships remain intact for a lifetime … and in the world as it is today many of these connections fall away over time. People change … they move … they alter their beliefs and values … and they drift away from things, including connections that were meaningful to them at a different time in their lives.

There are other connections that are more formal, requiring a deliberate decision to create and continue. Groups you belong to that you have chosen yourself exert a powerful influence on the Life Story you hold, and the sense of identity that generates. Some of the kinds of groups I have mentioned above are extremely meaningful when the decision is made to join them, and continue to be so as you mature and remain associated with them. For instance, one of the most influential kinds of groups a person can join is one that is contained within a closed environment, especially ones that represent life and death commitments or relationships in some meaningful way, e.g.: street and motorcycle gangs, an organized crime family or cartel, the military or law enforcement. First and foremost we are social beings and I would argue

that the process of identifying with the groups that you associate with, i.e.: the "Who We Are" part of your Life Story is unavoidable ...
it is as simple as recognizing that you are connected to others in some way, e.g.: a member of a family and the society that contains it.

"Who I Am ..."

All the stories about "Who We Are" that you hold onto become part of the story you hold about "Who I Am."

Beyond the "Who We Are" stories, there are also all the personal stories that shape your life, these are unique "Who I Am" stories about you as an individual. These stories include the historical events of your life ... the tribulations and thrills, the times you crashed and the times you celebrated ... the entirety of the historical record of you. We could call the historical stories of your life, "Who I Have Been" stories ... although these stories are always perceived as though the events they are representing from the past are being experienced in the present moment. "Who I Am" stories also include the things you believe and value ... about yourself, about others, about the world-at-large. They are also about your aspirations ... what you intend and desire ... and in the same way that there are historical stories, those about your future we could call "Who I Will Be" stories.

The totality of the stories you hold as the autobiographical narrative entitled "Your Life Story" is a mythological construct. When you create the story of your life, i.e.: "Your Life Story," you use mythic form to do it, and in so doing you create the great myth of your life. Each of us considers our life in a mythical, even legendary, way. For us our Life Story is epic, with moments of drama, comedy, joy, ecstasy, tragedy, terror and horror ... the totality of the story always greater than any single moment could hope to capture. Your Life Story is bigger than you are ... and yet it will always be smaller than the totality it represents, even when you exaggerate it ... via intention, inferiority or ignorance. The way you relate to the stories of your life can vary, and as they do they will have a different impact on you.

Regardless of the story you tell of your life, or how it is told, what most shapes your story is contained in the "WHO" you are being in the moment of the telling …and again in the hearing.

Ontology Trumps Epistemology …. "Ergo Sum Cogito"

The Terror And Thrill Of Discovery

"I remember one of the first times I realized I had a Life Story."

What made the moment I realized I had a Life Story distinct was my realization that my Life Story was just that … a story, not who I was or even necessarily real in any sense of representing reality beyond the story itself. It was in 1970, I was eleven years old, and I found my first "New Age" book. The book I found was about alternative lifestyles that I pulled from the shelves of the Newark Public Library Annex attached to my elementary school.

Having a small library attached to my school was very convenient, and it became one of my favorite places to visit. Looking at the book stacks was akin to peering into unknown universes of wonderment for me. I recognized those books waiting there in the stacks for me to read them as vehicles that would transport me beyond my limits growing up as a young boy in urban New Jersey … to other places and times I would never otherwise visit on my own. My favorites were non-fiction books about animals and natural history, the human body and mind, and scientific things like astronomy and the planet, and on occasion biographies.

As my reading deepened it expanded in range and breadth as well. I began to reach the limits of my small library's store of books on my favorite topics in the children's section, petitioned and got permission to go into the Junior Adult and Adult stacks, with supervision of course. I could read anything I wanted, as long as it was not about the forbidden topic … SEX! This was in the 1970s and that topic was becoming big for publishers. At that time, as a ten year old boy approaching eleven I never thought of it as a limitation. What I had found was the philosophy section, which in some intrinsic way called out to me instead … the more

CHAPTER TEN

esoteric the better. Much of what attracted my attention came from the Orient or the Far East, while some of the others things I was reading came from the Near East ... the Levant or as we more commonly refer to it today, the Middle East. What caught my attention most of all was martial arts philosophy, especially the writings of the modern Zen masters ... but I am getting ahead of myself.

The New Age book that exploded my world in 1970 came from the library adult book stacks. It was a book of descriptions about lifestyle choices people were making that were completely foreign to me. These descriptions included ideas about health and wellness, things like meditation and moxibustion I had never heard of before. There were descriptions of martial arts and yoga that were beyond anything I ever thought about before I read that book. However, there was also a suggestion that for some people these things were part of a spiritual or even religious path, this idea was utterly foreign to me.

As an eleven year old I knew about the religions of the people I encountered up to that point in my life. My own religious upbringing brought me into contact with a lot of Roman Catholics. I had Jewish friends and I knew their Jewish families. I also knew that there were other Christians like from friends I had at school and around the neighborhood ... Episcopalians, Methodists, Anglicans, Baptists and Pentecostals. We lived just a couple of blocks away from a large, beautiful Ukrainian Eastern Orthodox Catholic church so I knew about Orthodox Catholics, that were like Roman Catholics, but different. I had met and befriended a few Moslems and Hindus at school, so I knew those religions existed. But I had no idea that people would do things like meditation, forego all animal foods, or follow a prolonged fast as a kind of spiritual or religious practice.

As a child religion was a pretty clear concept ... G-d created heaven and earth, was omniscient and omnipotent, ruled from heaven with the angels, and watched over me and everyone else on the planet. I also imagined G-d at that time as a "Him" who was old and had a white beard ... you know the image if you have ever seen Michaelangelo's fresco, "The Creation of Adam," painted on the ceiling of the Sistine Chapel. There was no other consideration of what G-d could be, or the possibility that there were other gods plural. I thought that everyone prayed to the same G-d I did, and just went to different churches, temples or mosques to do it. I also had the sense that there might be different names for G-d or different languages to pray in, other than the English I was used to hearing, like the Italian my grandmother used when she prayed.

When I was reading the New Age book I had picked up in the library it hit me, "other people worship other gods, some of them worship many gods, and there are even some people who do not believe in G-d at all" … and there were people out there doing something entirely different that was like the prayer and worship I knew and understood, but not like I knew or understood it. Holy Moly! In that instant my entire worldview, or as the Germans say my "weltanschuung," was totally revised.

All of a sudden, in what seemed like one fell swoop, the world and what it contained as I knew it was shattered and replaced by something much, much bigger, and much more foreign than I could have imagined before that moment … and it was both terrifying and tempting beyond belief. I had to know what else was out there that no one had bothered to tell me about before I picked up that book. It was not just the difference in beliefs that shocked me, it was most of all the difference in practices - this went beyond going to church and praying.

My worldview had been challenged at times other than when I first encountered ideas about alternative lifestyles and religious practices than my own, but for some reason I could make those challenges fit into the framework of the world I knew. When I came across ideas about truly alternative lifestyles, that included ways of knowing about G-d and the Universe going beyond anything I knew or could have imagined, it just blew me away.

When I picked that book up off the shelf at the library and began reading it I faced a choice. One option was to accept the new information and update my beliefs based on it. If I did not, or could not, update my beliefs, I would have to reject all the new information I had encountered. Rejecting what I had read in that book meant I would have to retreat to the smaller, more familiar and comforting set of beliefs I already had, trusting those beliefs and finding a way to make them continue to work for me as they were. Without specifically or formally intending to at the time, I chose the first course of action … updating my beliefs.

In my ignorance I had chosen a life of adventure … **I had become an "Apprentice of Wonder."**

The shift I made was simple and profound. I accepted that the story I knew of the world, the Universe and my life in it was not the total story or the real story. I wanted to know what the "real story" was and set off to find it. That decision opened my eyes to an ever expanding sense of wonderment beyond what I had already known ...

I was open to the realization that I did not know much at all, and the willingness to suspend all I believed I knew to have a direct experience that went beyond "knowing."

Somehow at the age of eleven, once I had read the New Age book I had plucked from the shelves of my small public library, I knew that I did not have all the information I needed or wanted. I was compelled, by what seemed to be an irresistible force, to continue the adventure I had begun. The Call to Adventure was the decision I made to accept my own ignorance and extend beyond the limits of my own "knowing." I was fortunate in that I had already learned that there were ways to get information, and that the process of getting it could be wondrous itself.

I loved reading books, and so I avidly pursued that way of accumulating more of the information that might support me on my journey beyond myself. I also loved discussing what I was learning with others. Quickly I learned that I needed to have my discussions with adults, because virtually all the attempts I made were rejected when I tried to have those discussions with any of my friends close to my own age. One of the older guys I looked up to at the time took to calling me "Encyclopedia" ... both a compliment, and an insult. So I got it ... I was smart enough to keep the information I was chasing down and gathering close to the chest. I began sharing what I was discovering very selectively. I have found that this proved to be a good piece of learning worth continuing to this day.

Sometimes the less we share about our fascinations the easier it is to maintain them intact. At the very least, we must be selective about with whom we choose to share our deepest passions.

There are the exceptions to the rule of keeping your fascinations private and held close to the chest, e.g.: when you encounter someone who shares your interest with you. The most beneficial thing that can happen when you are hot on the heels of pursing your fascination is meeting someone who can take you much further into the adventure than you have been on your own.

Specifically, the most fortunate thing possible is actually meeting someone who is willing and able to become your Guide ... pointing you towards the mystery, walking you across the threshold, acting as your mentor while you learn how to navigate, and continuing to hold the space as sacred while all this happens ... at least until you can hold that space for yourself.

This is the process it takes to "become fully human" as Joseph Campbell referred to it. Instinctively I knew that Roye was such a Guide, someone who was able and willing to mentor me. Upon meeting him I realized I had met a kindred, elder soul who was much further along on the journey than I was, and I sensed that under the right conditions Roye could and would share with me the wonders he had found along the way.

Finding and connecting with others who were further along a path I was interested in than I was myself was a way of engaging the Adventure that was and remains near and dear to me. I found out I was really good at this early on in my life. Some of the martial arts teachers I had fit into this category, and "Bob the Dog Trainer" too. The ones I stayed with were not necessarily the first teachers I met. I had a powerful vetting strategy I learned to trust implicitly, and I did so without fail. I would enter into the "student" relationship completely open to what was present, literally willing to submit myself entirely to the learning experience. My initial strategy was to do what I was told, even if it did not make sense to me at the time. I trusted in five things that would serve to keep the path of wonder open and available to me ...

1. I did not know enough to know what made sense as I was learning, so it was best to find someone who did and model how they did it

2. My instincts and intuitions were good so I could trust that if something were really off I would recognize it and walk away

3. After the fact, as I reflected on what I was learning, I would be able to recognize if it was a match for me or not, and I could decide then to continue or to move on

4 There would always be other opportunities waiting for me to pursue, as long as I was willing to surrender, i.e.: letting go and giving up what I already had, to get what I did not have yet

5 Rather than retreating to the familiar, safe and comfortable, the future beckons most strongly when I left my past behind ... boldly and courageously stepping forth into the unknown

This strategy served me incredibly well. I found some brilliant teachers and models to learn from in each of the fields I pursued. Every brilliant teacher I had shared two specific qualities:

A. They were at a point in their own learning where they themselves were continuing to develop their own skills ... still peaking, even if they were already masterful

B. They were open and willing to share what they knew without limitation (to the extent that I was ready to learn what was on offer), even when they did not quite know how to do that

In the best cases I was able to find and learn from folks who also had incredible teaching skills. In my life I have only encountered this confluence of someone who was at the peak of their skills, had the willingness to share what they knew completely, and was a masterful teacher rarely ... with absolute confidence I can say just once, or now maybe twice. Yet when this combination is in place it is a magical experience. I was truly fortunate to meet Roye under these conditions, under his tutelage I was able to deliberately and intentionally choose who I wanted to become, access the sense of holding an identity that resonated ... and to make the changes to become that person.

Losing My Mind ... And Finding It Again

There is a variation on an old Sufi teaching tale about looking for things where they are not because "the light is better" that I used in my book **"State of Perfection: Your Hidden Code to Unleashing Personal Mastery"** to make the following point: most people go through their lives looking for what they most desire to be true of themselves where they are most familiar and comfortable, i.e.: where the light is better from their point of view.

Without retelling the whole tale here, it is about a drunken man who loses his keys and is looking for them when he is approached by a police officer, who enquires as to what the drunken man is doing. Once the police officer had been told that the man had lost his keys he offers to help. After much searching the policeman becomes a bit distraught and asks the man, "Are you sure you lost your keys?" to which the man, who is a bit annoyed by the question says to him, "Yes!" quite emphatically. The officer then asks him if he is sure that he lost them where they are looking for them, as there is no sign of them whatsoever. The man replied, "No, I lost them up there in the alley." Shocked the policeman asks him why they have spent so much time searching for them where they are not. The drunk responds by saying, "Because the light is better here."

For most people seeking something where they are unfamiliar and uncomfortable evokes a sense of unremitting cognitive dissonance. This is true even when what they are looking for is their essential self. Cognitive dissonance is the effect of dealing with the unknown, something that is beyond the range of one's current experience.

The most common response to cognitive dissonance is that it triggers the sympathetic pathway in the ANS (Autonomic Nervous System) to shut down in fear. Sometimes the response is simple avoidance, willfully choosing to ignore and disregard what is unknown, as though it does not exist. Other times there may be a full-blown flight response, creating the desire to run away from the disorienting stimulus … literally or figuratively. Many people freeze and are completely unable to act or even move in the face of the unknown. What remains nonetheless is that in each of these response patterns the disturbing stimulus remains despite one's best efforts to ignore it, run from it or freeze in the face of it.

Instead of remaining free to decide and then to follow up on their decisions, when faced with cognitive dissonance it is far more likely that unless someone is trained to respond otherwise they will look for someone to rescue them from whatever it is that has disrupted their "normal" experience. This pattern of avoidance and disowning one's personal responsibility to act, i.e.: their "respond-ability," is installed early on for most people. The pattern that limits or constrains respond-ability typically begins at home, and is continued throughout most formal schooling. There is an in-built premise of "learned helplessness" in the enculturation process prevalent in most social systems that all real expertise lies beyond the individual. The message engendered in school is that others know more than you do, or are more competent and capable than you are, and that you need someone with expertise to step in and save you. The message "you need to be saved" applies to just about every life experience where you do not yet have sufficient fluency to act on your own.

The idea that we are not good enough as we are is impressed upon us from the time we leave the womb. Instead of learning to trust ourselves we are taught and forced to learn what others believe we need to know and is good for us. We are told by our parents how to act and what to think, e.g.: This food is good for you ... this food is not ... and 'that' is not even food, despite the fact that others elsewhere eat it regularly and call it food 'over there' where they live. Then we go to school and are immediately taught that the teacher is the expert, and that in comparison to his or her expertise we know little to nothing. So we learn to look to experts for input, instead of relying on our own instincts, intuitions and investigations about learning for ourselves.

In many ways and places making mistakes in the name of learning is discouraged ... not only are we taught how we must do something, but we are also taught that we must do it the way we have been taught to do it. For instance, we go to doctors to heal us, often for the smallest malady before any attempt at healing or curing ourselves is undertaken ... even when the "cure" would require only some common sense on our part, e.g.: stay home and rest. We are taught that it is too risky to leave our health and wellbeing to our own care, and that only by following the advice of the expert can we hope to get and remain well. In virtually every area of our lives there are experts coming out of the woodwork.

Unfortunately, most experts do not guide us to our own innate way of knowing what is right for ourselves, or learning what we do not yet know. Instead, experts leap to giving us solutions and prescriptions for whatever ails us ... from personal distress, to relationship trials and tribulations, business dysfunction or just about any other aspect of our lives where we experience even momentary confusion or discomfort.

The insanity we face in our society is the delusion that we are not enough unto ourselves, either as individuals or collectively ... and that we need someone to "save us," some expert or agency, like the government, and we sacrifice the experience of our lives to their care in return.

The situation we face is that options for both sanity and insanity reside in our Life Story, the autobiographical narrative that defines and guides us in every moment of our lives. Typically, before we even know that we have a Life Story, it is wrested away from us and in the control of others, then we become what it tells us we should be. Most often this leads to massive discontent, internal angst that arises from a sublime awareness that we are not living our own life.

Instead of living our own life, when we are not in charge of our Life Story we are living a life that has been imposed and bestowed upon us by others. Instead of having the experience of our life, we wind up living according to other people's rules, living in relation to their laws, doing what they expect of us, fulfilling a duty they have installed in us ... and all at the cost of becoming ourselves.

We are always living in alignment with a story, EXCEPT THAT IT IS NOT NECESSARILY OUR STORY.

In the standard arrangement we do not perceive that we are not living our own story. Far too often, the story we are living is one that others want us to incorporate and obey, because it serves them and the system they are trapped within ... and they have no choice but to ensnare us in it as well. The awful joke of course is that they are also living a story that is not their own, it is a story that is passed on and perpetuated in exactly the same way they impose it upon and install it in us.

Often, when the deep knowing that would normally inform our Life Story is out of sync with experience, a sense of foreboding that this is NOT the way it is supposed to be descends upon us. We are NOT

CHAPTER TEN

designed and destined to drone on in our lives in the service of the system, while we ignore the call to Adventure and sacrifice ourselves.

First, we must perceive that we are living in relation to a story to even have a chance to do anything about it. Then we must choose to take hold of our story to suss out the themes that direct and guide our perceptions, decisions, actions and the results we create in our lives. To suss out our story we need the key or the code that unlocks it for us. The mechanism that unlocks the story ... separating what is obvious at the surface level as content and revealing to us what is hidden in the deep structure ... is mythic form. When you become aware of the deep structure of your story you can begin asking the hard questions about whether the story you are living is in fact your own ... only then can you begin to shape it to your will, to discover your destiny and to begin to "**Have The Experience of Your Life.**"

When I got to this point in my own journey, magnificently guided to the realization of the presence and impact of my Life Story, I became aware that it was held deep in my body. The Life Story exists and is expressed in every facial expression, gesture, movement, and in the way we hold ourselves. I learned that we contain the source and storehouse of our Life Story in our bodies. If I wanted to take control of how my story was playing out I needed to learn how my body held and told that story. This was the gift that I received in the journey to becoming fully myself, to own the complete embodied awareness of how I am in any and every moment ... responding to the events of my life as they emerge and are happening.

In some systems this way of operating, being present to the unfolding, emergent moment might be call "Mindfulness" - and that is very close to what I am suggesting, i.e.: to remain ever mindful. However, there are a few deep distinctions in the MythoSelf Process that inform and shape the way I remain present, and in the way I lead others to becoming and remaining present as well.

The primary distinction in the MythoSelf Process is contained in the idea of experiencing life, and all the events that comprise it systemically, i.e.: in whole-form, connected to everything else as an ever unfolding singularity ... which creates the essential foundation of W-learning (whole-form learning) and W-communication (whole-form communication). The most significant aspect of this particular distinction is recognizing the interconnectedness of all things and the recursive nature of cybernetic loops present in any system. In cybernetic systems one thing informs another and so on in an endless chain of feedback and iteration. In human cybernetic systems the reverberatations of interaction continue between actors and agents within the system without end, even continuing post-generationally from parent to child, and in organizations from one regime to the next. Fully getting the system in this way, or "groking*"it, means getting that human systems are dynamic, non-linear, non-sequential and therefore not necessarily deterministic, so you must choose your response carefully with regard to the outcomes and consequences you intend to create.

Another distinction has to do with the emphasis on attending to somatic awareness and communication, i.e.: somatic intelligence. Somatic intelligence begins by remaining in touch with and tuned into your own body, recognizing when we are in the presence of others that we are always experiencing them somatically as well as in every other possible way. Somatic intelligences is about allowing the signals in your body to inform you at an intuitive, if not instinctive, level about how to respond, including choosing the signals you send and want to be sending to others. At its best the human somatic system is a finely tuned and responsive tool, able to perceive and respond to data in the environment far faster than we are able to cognitively perceive, interpret, cogitate, make decisions about and respond to what we are experiencing consciously. Our somatic system may be our finest instrument in making sense of and responding to the world around us, including others we encounter in it.

A third distinction of the model is the aesthetic focus on sensory-based data and sensory integration to filter the data you perceive in making sense of it, e.g.: using the aesthetic qualities of sensuousness, beauty and pleasure as ways of knowing the world. Using an aesthetic orientation the wine we drink is its bouquet and flavor ... the feel of it on our tongue, against our pallet and the sense of it sliding through our throat as we swallow. In the same way our lover is the sight of his or her face, the sound of their voice, the feel of their touch and the smell and taste of them in our nostrils and on our lips. Each experience we have like this, when we are deeply and profoundly connected with our own experience of being brings with it a quality of sensuality that is unmistakable, along with our response and appraisal. When experiences are held purely aesthetically we are only able to respond to by moving toward or away, wanting more or less ... seldom if ever remaining neutral or uncertain, except perhaps to "grok*" the experience ever more fully and robustly in our next encounter.

Without getting too metaphysical about it, within the MythoSelf Process model every event is perceived as part of a larger system. Someone trained in the MythoSelf Process model always strives to remain aware that there are limits to their perception and to act accordingly. There are always things that we do not and cannot know that are impacting and influencing the system and our immediate experience of it. MythoSelf Process training forces a sorting pattern that is organized around remaining aware of the larger system that contains and influences events as they are happening. Becoming aware of the system-at-large extends your reach in space and time relative to the events you are experiencing. So, in summation someone using the MythoSelf Process model thinks in terms of what can be known, what is unknown (but could be known), and what is unknowable that is impacting their experience and visa-versa ...

The Known, Unknown and Unknowable - An Example:

- ✓ Whenever you are speaking with someone else you know what is happening between you and them, that you can and do choose to track, e.g.: what they say, what they do, what is happening in the environment around you ...
- ✓ When you are speaking with someone else you are unlikely to know everything they did, everywhere they have been or everyone they met before you, the entirety of their personal history, every intention they hold about everything that is important to them, their agenda or aspirations ... all this and more may be unknown to you
- ✓ In speaking with someone there are also things that cannot be known by you, e.g.: events happening elsewhere that might impact what you decide and do ... environmental events, economic events, war, transportation delays ... all that has happened in the past and what may happen in the future that may impact the decisions you are making now and the actions you take ... i.e.: in the space and time you currently occupy these things remain unknowable to you

Yet, despite the fact that there are things you know, things you know you do not know and unknowable things, remaining present in the system that contains you and the events you experience, allows you to remain flexible and resilient as new information becomes present ... constantly updating your Life Story and your sense of being as you do, creating new possibilities and opportunities to pursue. Even when things go pear shaped, or the system is "FUBAR" ... you can remain centered and able to act within the swirling chaos that surrounds you.

The ability to ...

A. **Remain aware of what is happening as it unfolds and to new information as it emerges**

B. **Update your story as you hold and experience it to incorporate the new data ...**

is the basis for what I refer to as being sane, i.e.: accounting for the information that is actually present in the context, and responding to it in a way that is aligned with what you want, who you are and who you intend to become. Furthermore, as human beings we experience a singularity in ourselves as embodied beings, i.e.: we are our lived experiences, and we experience our lives in and through our bodies. I like to point to the simple and evident idea that, **"Wherever I go there I am!"** ... meaning we cannot have an experience without our bodies being present (even when we are not present to our bodies). We even experience purely imaginal events as though they are embodied. Whatever we want or need to update in our Life Story, we must update in an embodied way ... we need to change the experience we have with and in our bodies, if we want or need to change the experience we have in and of our life.

As a result of many years of studying with Roye, and many more years afterwards continuing to learn on my own, I became present to my life and the expectations I have about who I most want to be in every moment I am alive. The trick is the realization that I cannot have the life I want as an "idea" or a "mental projection." If I want to live my life fully, I have to live it fully in each moment … wherever I am, on my own and with others … including, how I experience and hold it in my body.

**To regain my sanity, I had to go beyond "thinking" and re-learn the "trick" that every child knows about experiencing the events of their lives fully: living life as it happens …
body, mind and soul.**

Children are great teachers before they become corrupted by the systems that contain them. Every child, before a certain age, lives joyfully as long as they are not in distress. When a child is in distress they seek to change the circumstances they are experiencing to accommodate themselves, and not themselves to accommodate the circumstances. As soon as the circumstances are changed to accommodate them, e.g.: they are fed when they are hungry, they are clothed or wrapped in a blanket when they are cold, they are held if they are lonely, afraid or just want to be loved … they immediately return to being at peace with the world. All it takes for a child to be fully satisfied and joyful is to be at peace and content. For children there is no consideration of being successful or attainment of any kind. Rather than striving for externally qualified experience they simply opt for satisfaction and joyfulness. The secret possessed by children when they emerge from the womb into the world is the skeleton key to living life fully and becoming ourselves. The secret to living life fully and joyfully could not be simpler …

**"Be and remain present to ourselves,
and the world that contains us."**

As infants this is as simple as allowing ourselves to experience what is happening as we become aware of it emerging, and responding to our bodily demands and desires. As we continue developing it includes becoming aware of who we are by learning to notice our fascinations and what tugs at us to become what we will become … the mass of our future exerting its unavoidable gravitational pull on us.

At some point it also becomes evident to us that we are neither alone, nor the center of the Universe unto ourselves, and we must include others in our experience of ourselves. This moment, when we lose our sense of being solely at the center of the Universe, is a quantum realization for most people ... and one that many people never fully grasp. Or course this means that most people never fully grow up. We can feel the experience of others in how they affect us with regard to our embodied experience of them, and of ourselves in relation to them. In the same way we can feel the urges of our own body towards or away from them. The embodied experience of others applies equally to love and hate, delight or disgust, empathy or apathy ... we know these things in response to others because we feel them in ourselves.

The feelings we have, about ourselves ... about others ... about the world-at-large ... the events of our lives ... and the way we express those feelings, writes and re-writes our Life Story. This is true regardless of whether we are referring to micro-muscular responses that are the precursors to our expressions, gestures, movement, postural changes or gross motor movements like laughing, clenching our fists, talking, walking or feverishly dancing out the expression of our "*joie de vivre*."

Our stories are contained in the embodiment of our experiences, and the in the way we express ourselves as a result of what we embody. When you recognize the power of your Life Story ... and the ability you have to shape it by virtue of how you choose to live in relation to it, you become free to truly begin having ...

"The Experience of Your Life"

After many years of searching I found that the skeleton key to unlocking profound satisfaction and joy in my life was as simple as letting go of the conceptions and mentations about my life, and beginning to live fully within it "as is" in each moment. I shifted my attention from thinking about and intellectualizing my life, to taking each moment ... each person ... each event ... as they come. I now accept and reside in the knowing that remaining aware of how I am feeling, using aesthetic form in the place of rational premises, consciously choosing to be present to and in my body ... all guide me in knowing if I am closer to or further away from myself as I know I want to be and towards who I want to be becoming. In this way "knowing" and "being" collide and become one.

CHAPTER TEN

I am residing in the Adventure of my life ... on the Journey to Becoming Fully Human ... ... finally, after losing my mind and finding myself ... embodied again ... I have become, and I remain sane ... an Apprentice of Wonder!

Ergo Sum Cogito ... Sentio Ergo Sum
(I am, therefore I think ... I sense therefore I am)

*groking/grok: to understand profoundly and intuitively, coined by American author Robert A. Heinlein, first known use - 1961 in "Stranger in a Strange Land"

Epilogue:

"All we have to decide is what to do with the time that is given us."

- J.R.R. Tolkien
The Fellowship of the Ring

EPILOGUE

Living in Wonder

Identity is a powerful thing, and it is contained within and by your Life Story. Change your story and you begin to change your life. An essential thing to remember is that it is just a story of course, and that the way you tell the story determines who you are as you do, and who you will be as you hear yourself telling it.

One of my former students, let's call him Dr. D., was a practicing physician, a qualified Plastic Surgeon, a skillful hypnotist and a licensed and certified NLP Trainer with the Society of NLP when I met him. He had been around the block with many NLP Trainers, and had a ton of experience with many teachers, including some famous and renowned ones. When he encountered the model as I was teaching it with my partner, and later wife, Nancy, he immediately realized the transformational power it offered.

The doctor had the unique ability when he found something that fit for him, to decide on the spot to let go of anything that would prevent him from capturing what was being offered fully and completely. Once Dr. D. had been led through the MythoSelf Process and experienced the "Ready State" that becomes present as a result he said, "Is that it? This is all I have to do to keep this?!??!" and he did. That experience alone reset him on his own journey. Shortly afterward he left the practice of medicine to pursue this calling with me on a full-time basis.

The good doctor spent many years learning with me, diligently studying what I did in the training room, in private work I did with him personally and in his own work with private clients. At first it was pure "copying the master" as I had done with Roye, literally replicating as best he could what I was doing. He would often video tape my presentations, or client work, and the next time I would see him he would have modeled what I had done, and was replicating some of it himself ... often to the point of using the exact words I had spoken verbatim.

Eventually the doctor began developing his own style under my direction, supervision and mentoring, spending many years learning and then teaching alongside me. By the time we had completed our dance of learning together he was a masterful facilitator and trainer of the model I had developed, the MythoSelf Process. He was one of only two people I ever formally certified as a Master Trainer of the model ... a high compliment indeed, and one I believe that he had earned and was well deserved.

"Joseph is one of the few people who I've ever met who is a master of what he teaches ... is willing to share all he's learned and knows ... and beyond that is willing and capable of teaching others what he's doing so that they can learn how to do it for themselves.", was something Dr. D. often said of me to others when he introduced me to them.

The doctor pointed to the same idea I am sharing here ... it is one thing to know how to do what you do ... i.e: being an expert, master or even genius in what you do ... but it is another thing entirely to know how to teach it to others in a way that as a result they would become masterful. Dr. D's comments were among the highest compliments I ever received, from someone who had reason to know of that which he spoke. By the time he shared his opinion with me I respected what he had accomplished himself, independent what he had to say about me.

The doctor's story of pursuing his fascination is a classic tale of encountering and choosing the adventure. He was by all accounts already accomplished when he first met me. As a gifted physician he could have easily remained in the profession of plastic surgery, and lived a comfortable life, become highly respected and might even have become wealthy if he so chose. Yet, when Dr. D. encountered NLP something began to shift, something stirred inside of him by his own account. Then when he first met me, and Nancy and I did some work with him in a training he attended, he made an "on the spot" decision to pursue what it was that we were offering without hesitation, fully committing himself to it. He recognized that something deeply resonated for him, and like when I had first met Roye. The doc had the internal awareness that he was in the presence of someone who could and would lead him further into his adventure than he had been able to go on his own. It was also in that moment his entire Life Story shifted as well.

When Dr. D. made the decision to pursue studying the MythoSelf Process model with me he was no longer who he had been the moment before. In part his ability to make this decision to fully commit, and to leave behind the old identity and all it represented, was the essential quality that allowed him to become masterful. That decision meant giving up the identity of being a physician, an NLP Trainer or anything else he had been or could have chosen, and choosing instead to become a MythoSelf Trainer in that moment, before he even knew that he could be one. Rather than choosing to remain as he had known himself to be, or to rest on his accomplishments, he went on to earn the privilege of becoming, not just a MythoSelf Trainer, but as I already said, one of only two MythoSelf Master Trainers I have ever certified.

While Dr. D's story is now more than a decade old the fundamental learning and lessons still apply as much as ever. For instance, much of Dr. D's achievement had to do with his innate capability to succeed and his dedication to doing so once he had made up his mind. As a result of the choice he made, the learning he pursued, and his success in becoming masterful on the path he chose, the doc built a successful practice as a MythoSelf Facilitator and Trainer … working with clients local to him and abroad as well. He eventually began presenting MythoSelf professional training internationally, running a MythoSelf Facilitator Certification Training program in Spain with a partner he made for himself there. More importantly Dr. D. reformed his Life Story and began manifesting the life that he desired.

It could be argued that living his life fully had eluded the good doctor before he came to fully owning the Adventure of his life and updating his Life Story, in part through experiencing and becoming masterful in the MythoSelf Process.

It is profoundly magical to choose to have what I call, "The Experience Of Your Life" … i.e.: choosing not to remain stuck in the life designed by others for you … and worst, imposed upon you by virtue of the past you have already lived. In some ways it could be said that choosing to leave behind the past and choosing to live for the future is an amazing talent that can be learned. However, it would probably be more accurate to say that for many people who "choose" to live fully into their own life, the choice is not so much a choice as it is a kind of compulsion.

The real "choice" is choosing to pursue the story that has been following you around all your life.

Even if you have chosen to turn your back on it, either completely or from time to time, your Life Story will not be denied. You must come to terms with your Life Story, accept it … acknowledge it … fully and completely assimilate it … so you can live it … or it will haunt you to death. As Joseph Campbell said, "The call denied becomes crisis." I can tell you from personal experience … based on work I have done with clients and in my own life as well … that the crisis is rarely pleasant. It can come in the form of physical, mental, emotional or spiritual distress or disease, but it will always have at its core a mythological origin.

Your Life Story is an organic, living thing and it demands your attention. Try as you might the story will become manifest in one form or another. So the choice is either to contain and define your Life Story or have it contain and define you. Encountering your Life Story takes learning and skill, heck my story about Dr. D. is a supreme example. He was extraordinarily bright and capable to begin with, and it still took him half a decade to get "IT."

My own story has been similar, hearing the Call and pursuing the Adventure, and it has been going on consistently and consciously for more than thirty years as I write these words … living my Life Story has become my life's work.

My life as an "Apprentice of Wonder" has been and remains about being present to where the wonder resides … regardless of where the wonder takes me.

May the wonder take you as well.

Buon Viaggio and Buona Fortuna … Joseph Riggio, Ph.D

Afterword:

"There are only four questions of value in life, Don Octavio.

What is sacred?
Of what is the spirit made?
What is worth living for, and ...
What is worth dying for?

The answer to each is the same: only love."

- Don Juan DeMarco
From the film *"Don Juan DeMarco"*

AFTERWORD: JOSEPH RIGGIO, Ph.D.

[**AUTHOR'S NOTE:** *While I recognize that it is unusual for a book to have an Epilogue and an Afterword, and even more so for the Afterword to be written by the author, but this has been an unusual book, so here goes ...*]

I started the journey with you as a reader with a quote in my Preface taken from "A Few Good Men" by Aaron Sorkin where Colonel Nathan R. Jessup tells Liuetenant Daniel Kaffee that he "*can't handle the truth*" ...

In my own experience and observation most people can neither handle the truth, nor do they really want it ...
- Joseph Riggio, Ph.D.

If you are not sure you are ready for the truth it would probably be best to close the book here and now, and go on your way "as is" ... however if you think you are up for it I do have a few more parting words.

Beyond Paradox: "Everything Is Really Nothing" ...

To you my dear reader I offer this update to Dr. D's story to share that there are no guarantees in life ... but, maybe, just maybe ... as we conclude our time here together you will have come to accept two things:

1. It is ALL just a story, and
2. You CAN "handle the truth"

This next bit may be for you the real threshold to adventure that Joseph Campbell talks about ... or the beginning of becoming an Apprentice of Wonder as like to think about it ... so whether or not you continue reading is up to you. Either way here is where I take my final adieu and part ways with you for a while as your humble (or not so humble, as the case may be) guide on the Journey of life.

The Never-Ending Story Continues ...

I just wanted to articulate a final, final point beyond the Epilogue where reasonable authors are supposed to make their final points and take their leave.

It has come to my attention that Dr. D. has recently again updated his story after spending more than a decade on the elusive search to find himself spent learning, practicing and presenting the MythoSelf Process from me, with me, alongside me and on his own.

As I understand it now, the story goes that he has decided he was wrong for all of those years, i.e.: the MythoSelf Process was not the panacea he thought it might have been ... in fact he may have been deluding himself to believe it at all. According to the most recent story it all may have been a ruse ... a way to seduce him into a cult ... by the way a rather curious cult that never charged him following the first workshop he attended for most of the ten years of learning, training or mentoring he received. A cult led by the possessive madman he supposedly uncovered that he freely walked away from and easily abandoned without resistance. Nor did he bother to look back on those he left behind when he had decided it no longer served his current needs or outcomes.

It seems the good doctor decided to abdicate any personal responsibility for his choices and/or actions in the course of the ten plus years he spent within the MythoSelf community. He has chosen to play the blame game instead, pointing a crooked finger away from himself and towards others despite the gains he achieved from making those original choices, and taking the action associated with the decisions he had made. Some of the gains during that time included creating a major shift that allowed him to rebuild his life, achieving a new level of freedom, recognition and respect, becoming a mentor and guide for others, and securing an income doing work that he loved.

I have been told that it is common in profound learning with a mentor, that the apprentice often must create a separation from the master to continue their own evolution - similar to "killing the parent" that is necessary for the adolescent to mature to adulthood. This theme is common in the mythological literature as well, as part of the hero's tale, a crucial aspect of undertaking the adventure and being on the journey. For instance in the film, StarWars, Luke leaves Dagobah despite Yoda's protestation that he is not ready. The apprentice shuns the master and in some ways only begins the true journey to becoming a master himself after he has made the decision to leave and find his own way.

In the old days there was a period of time, after the apprentice leaves the master, spent journeying around, meeting and learning from other masters. In order for the apprentice to pursue this path however they needed two things to be in place, a letter of acknowledgement or some other sort of verification from the master they had served of their readiness to undertake the journey, and the ability to make the separation required to leave. In a formal apprentice/master arrangement this happens as a matter of course. Without this formal arrangement it can be more troublesome. Sometimes it seems the apprentice feels the need to create separation by negating that which has taken them to where they now find themselves and smashing the pedestal they have built under the person who helped them get there. For what it is worth, I understand the psychic blow that comes with the realization that we are all only human.

When it was time I also found a need to create a separation from my mentor, Roye. While I never made a public spectacle of it, there was a time where my frustration and disappointment in discovering Roye's humanity and fallibility bordered on rage. I wanted and expected him to be superhuman, beyond any human failing. In my case I accepted that my festering rage was a product of my own projections. My disappointment had little to nothing to do with Roye, despite his human limitations and foibles, which much like myself he surely had in spades. While he was not without fault, Roye helped me to see myself and the world around me in ways I had been blind to before. In fact the only reasonable thing to say would be that before Roye's teaching and guidance I would not even have been capable of creating the separation from him that occurred, or the return back again as a peer and colleague.

In my case I returned to a long and fruitful relationship with Roye after a short hiatus apart feeling very much an equal on my own path. Yet, despite leaving as a Journeyman and returning as a Master, I have an ongoing sense of humility and gratitude for the gifts that came to me in the many years of learning with Roye, and the many years of collegial friendship that followed. It remains a truism that we must each find our own way, all part of our story as we create it and that in turn creates us as we know and experience ourselves to be. For what it's worth I wish Dr. D. only the best, may he find his Satori and Nirvana this time around, as I assume his search continues … alas, I am sad to report, this time around without my guidance, company or affection on the journey.

An Uneasy Ending …

There is one particularly unreasonable consideration I want you to have as I close this book with you as my reader.

As a result of what I have written, and the way you have read it, you may have come to a conclusion that I think that stories, and in particular your Life Story is important.

Well, in fact, I do not believe it … not even one tiny bit!

> **"I don't think that your Life Story –
> or any story for that matter is important …
> because, I don't think our stories are real!"**

Of course, your Life Story is as real as any other story, and compared to most stories is remarkably important to you … who you have been, who you are now and who you are becoming. The main thing that I have been pointing to over and over throughout this entire book is that nothing is real except as we make it so, and only as important to us as that.

Once we get over ourselves, and give up our self importance, we can begin to recognize the illusion that we are important as well. It would be fair to say that we are only as "important" or "real" as we make ourselves out to be … and no more than that.

Real is as much an illusion as anything else … including the reality of your Life Story. The reason you might want to do the work to get to your Life Story … to unfold it, embrace it, reshape it and make it your own … is so that you can finally give it up once and for all.

AFTERWORD

**The real trick in life is getting to "Nothing" ...
the place where everything is just what it is ...
and every moment begins again anew.**

There really is nothing to do or get, and therefore nothing to have or to hold onto either ... least of all knowledge or understanding ... just let it all go.

While, as I say, I realize this may be unreasonable, nonetheless when you come to the position where you get it is all just a story, and you can make it up as you go, you are free to do just that ... and you might as well make up a great story since you are going to have one anyway.

Like the famous quote by the famous Irish playwright, George Bernard Shaw:

"The reasonable man adapts himself to the conditions that surround him ... the unreasonable man adapts surrounding conditions to himself ... all progress depends on the unreasonable man."

... 'seems to me that being unreasonable is the beginning of most things that I have come to think of as worthwhile doing.

Going Beyond Paradox: "All Things That Begin Must End"

In closing am reminded of the last scene in the movie, "Don Juan DeMarco" with Johnny Depp and Marlon Brando having found a story that freed them both ... and in the end/beginning again we find them dancing, frolicking and kissing the ones they love on a beach somewhere in time.

It has been Don Juan DeMarco's philosophy on life that I hoped to have been able to impart to you ... if only just a bit and for the little while in time we have shared together here ...

"By seeing beyond what is visible to the eye. Now there are those, of course, who do not share my perceptions, it's true. When I say that

all my woman are dazzling beauties, they object. The nose of this one is too large; the hips of another, they are too wide; perhaps the breasts of a third, they are too small. But I see these women for how they truly are... glorious, radiant, spectacular, and perfect, because, I am not limited by my eyesight. Women react to me the way that they do, Don Octavio, because they sense that I search out the beauty that dwells within until it overwhelms everything else. And then they cannot avoid their desire, to release that beauty and envelope me in it. So, to answer your question, I see as clear as day that this great edifice in which we find ourselves is your villa. It is your home. And as for you, Don Octavio DeFlores, you are a great lover like myself, even though you may have lost your way and your accent. Shall I continue?"

- Don Juan DeMarco (as played by Johnny Depp) spoken to Don Octavio (as played by Marlon Brando), from "Don Juan DeMarco" 1994, written by Jeremy Levin, with respect to Lord Byron

What a great story!

Joseph Riggio, Ph.D.
Princeton, New Jersey 2013

PS - So, what's beyond the paradox?

Simply this ...

Love.

Why not save that idea for another story or two, shall we?

So, y'all come back now, ya' hear!

Further Resources:

"We must let go of the life we have planned, so as to accept the one that is waiting for us."
- Joseph Campbell

Recommended Reading:

Business, Cognitive Science & Decision Making:

Paul Eckman

Telling Lies: Clues to Deceit in the Marketplace, Politics and Marriage: W.W. Norton & Company, 1985
Emotions Revealed: Understanding Faces and Feelings: Times Books, 2003
Darwin and Facial Expression: A Century of Research in Review: Malor Books, 2006

Randy W. Green

Decisions, Decisions: How to Get Off the Fence and Choose What's Best for You!: Lyons Press, 2010

Gary Klein

Sources of Power: How People Make Decisions: The MIT Press, 1999
Streetlights and Shadows: Searching for the Keys to Adaptive Decision Making: A Bradford Book, 2011

Joseph Riggio

Towards a Theory of Transpersonal Decision Making in Human Systems: Universal Publishers, 2005

Joseph Riggio, Lee B. Salz, Jeb Blount, et al

Business Guide to Small Business Success: Business Expert Publishing, 2011

Joseph Riggio, Warren Bennis, Sen. George Mitchell, et al

Leadership: Helping Others to Succeed: Insight Publishing 2012

Joseph Riggio, Ken Blanchard, Deepak Chopra, et al

Roadmap to Success: Insight Publishing 2012

General Science & Neuroscience:

David Bohm

Wholeness and the Implicate Order: Routledge, 1980
Thought As A System: Routledge, 1994

Gygorgy Buzsaki

Rhythms of the Brain: Oxford University Press, 2011

Nicholas Humphrey

The Inner Eye: Social Intelligence in Evolution: Oxford University Press, 2003
Seeing Red: A Study in Consciousness: Belknap Press, 2009
Soul Dust: The Magic of Consciousness: Princeton University Press, 2011

Masao Ito

The Cerebellum: Brain for an Implicit Self: FT Press, 2011

Roger Lewin & Irving Dardik

Making Waves: Irving Dardik and His Superwave Principal: Rodale Books, 2005

Daniel Siegel

The Developing Mind: How Relationships and The Brain Interact To Shape Who We Are: The Guilford Press, 2001

Jeffrey M. Schwartz and Sharon Begley

The Mind and the Brain: Neuroplasticity and the Power of Mental Force: Harper Collins, 2003

Olaf Sporns

Networks of the Brain: MIT Press, 2010

Human Development, Psychology & Psychotherapy:

Susanne Cook-Grueter

Postautonomous Ego Development: A Study of Its Nature and Measurement: Integral Publishers, 2010

Susanne Cook-Greuter, Dalmar Fisher, Erica Foldy, Alain Gauthier William R. Torbert

Action Inquiry: The Secret of Timely and Transforming Leadership: Ingram Publisher Services, 2004

Susanne Cook-Grueter & Melvin Miller

Transcendence and Mature Thought in Adulthood: Rowman & Littlefield Publishers, 1994
Creativity, Spirituality, and Transcendence: Paths to Integrity and Wisdom in the Mature Self: Elsevier Science, 1999

Bradford Keeney

Aesthetics of Change: The Guilford Press, 2002

Jane Loevinger

Ego Development: Conceptions and Theories: Jossey-Bass, 1976

Angela Pfaffenberger

The Postconventional Personality: State University of New York Press, 2011

Robert Anton Wilson

Prometheus Rising: New Falcon Press, 1983
Quantum Psychology: New Falcon Press, 1990

Linguistics, Anthropology and Philosophy:

David Abram

The Spell of the Sensuous: Vintage, 1997

Gregory Bateson

Steps to an Ecology of Mind: University of Chicago Press, 1972
Mind and Nature: Bantam Books, 1980

Edward T. Hall

Beyond Culture: Anchor Books, 1976
The Hidden Dimension: Anchor Books, 1990

Mark Johnson

The Body in the Mind: The Bodily Basis of Meaning, Imagination and Reason: University of Chicago Press, 1990
The Meaning of the Body: Aesthetics of Human Understanding: University of Chicago Press, 2007

George Lakoff and Mark Johnson

Metaphors We Live By: University of Chicago Press, 1980
Philosophy In The Flesh: Basic Books, 1999

John Searle

Mind, Language and Society: Philosophy in the Real World: Basic Books, 2000

Paul Watzlawick

How Real Is Real?: Vintage, 1977
The Situation Is Hopeless, But Not Serious: W.W. Norton & Company, 1993
The Language of Change: Elements of Therapeutic Communication: W.W. Norton & Company, 1993

Ludwig Wittgenstein

Philosophical Investigations: Blackwell Publishing, 1953

Mythology & Spirituality:

Joseph Campbell

The Hero With A Thousand Faces: Princeton Press, 1949
Reflections on the Art of Living: A Joseph Campbell Companion: Harper Perennial, 1995

Joseph Campbell and Stanley Keleman

Myth and the Body: A Colloquy With Joseph Campbell: Center Press, 1999

Carlos Castaneda

The Teachings of Don Juan: A Yaqui Way of Knowledge: University of California, 1968
A Separate Reality: Further Conversations With Don Juan: Simon & Schuster, 1971
The Journey To Ixtlan: Simon & Schuster, 1972
The Fire From Within: Washington Square Press, 1971

Mircea Eliade

The Sacred and The Profane: The Nature of Religion: Hardcore Brace, 1959

Jed McKenna

Spiritual Enlightenment: The Damnedest Thing: Wisefool Press, 2002
Spiritually Incorrect Enlightenment: Wisefool Press, 2004
Spiritual Warfare: Wisefool Press, 2005

Alan Watts

The Wisdom of Insecurity: Pantheon, 1951
The Book: On the Taboo Against Knowing Who You Are: J. Cape, 1969

Ken Wilber

No Boundary: Eastern and Western Approaches to Personal Growth: Shambala 2001

Staurt Wilde

Life Was Never Meant to Be a Struggle: Hay House, 1995
The Quickening: Hay House, 1995
Whispering Winds of Change: Hay House, 1995
Silent Power: Hay House, 1998

NLP & Hypnosis:

Richard Bandler:

Magic In Action: Meta Publications, 1985
Using Your Brain for a Change: Real People Press, 1985
Time for a Change: Meta Publications 1993

Richard Bandler and John Grinder

Structure of Magic Vol. 1: Meta Publications, 1975
Patterns of the Hypnotic Techniques of Milton H. Erickson, Vol. 1: Meta Publications, 1975
Structure of Magic Vol. 2: Science and Behavior Books, 1976
Frogs into Princes: Real People Press, 1979
Trance-formations: Real People Press 1980

Richard Bandler and Garner Thompson

The Secrets of Being Happy: The Technology of Hope, Health and Harmony: IM Press Incorporated, 2011

Richard Bandler and John LaValle

Persuasion Engineering: Meta Publications, 1996

Richard Bandler and Will McDonald

An Insider's Guide to Sub-Modalities: Meta Publications 1989

Dave Elman

Hypnotherapy: Westwood Publishing Company, 1984

Milton H. Erickson & Ernest Rossi

Hypnotic Realities: The Induction of Clinical Hypnosis and Forms of Indirect Suggestion: John Wiley & Sons, Inc., 1975
Experiencing Hypnosis: Therapeutic Approaches to Altered States: Irvington Publishing, 1981
Healing in Hypnosis (Vol. 1): Irvington Publishers, 1983
Life Reframing in Hypnosis (Vol. 2): Irvington Publishing, 1984
Mind-Body Communication in Hypnosis (Vol.3): Irvington Publishing, 1987
Creative Choice in Hypnosis (Vol. 4): Irvington Publishing, 1991

John Grinder and Carmen Bostic St. Clair

Whispering In The Wind: John Grinder and Carmen Bostic St. Clair, 200

John Grinder and Judith DeLozier

Turtles All The Way Down: Grinder, DeLozier and Assoc., 1987

Jay Haley

Uncommon Therapy: The Psychiatric Technique of Miltion H. Erickson, M.D.: W.W. Norton & Company, 1993

Ronald Havens

The Wisdom of Milton H. Erickson: The Complete Volume: Crown House Publishing, 2005

Joseph Riggio

State of Perfection: Your Hidden Code to Unleashing Personal Mastery: I.M. Press, 2012

Joseph Riggio and Henrik Wenoe

Do What You Do Best, Vol. 2: Acuity World Press, 2011

Sidney Rosen

My Voice Will Go With You: The Teaching Tales of Milton H. Erickson: W.W. Norton & Company, 1991

Lee Wallas

Stories for the Third Ear: Using Hypnotic Fables in Psychotherapy: W.W. Norton & Company, 1985

Henrik Wenoe

Do What You Do Best, Vol. 1: Acuity World Press, 2009

Somatics:

F.M. Alexander

The Use of the Self: E.P. Dutton, 1932

Moshe Feldenkrais

Body Awareness as Healing Therapy: The Case of Nora: Harper & Row, 1977
The Elusive Obvious: Meta Publications, 1981
The Potent Self: A Study of Spontaneity and Compulsion: Harper & Row, 1985

Thomas Hanna

Somatics: Reawakening the Mind's Control of Movement, Flexibility and Health: De Capo Press, 1988
The Body of Life: Creating New Pathways for Sensory Awareness and Fluid Movement: Healing Arts Press, 1993

Stanley Keleman

Human Ground: Center Press, 1975
Your Body Speaks Its Mind: Center Press 1981
Somatic Reality: Center Press, 1982
Embodying Experience: Forming a Personal Life: Center Press, 1987
Emotional Anatomy: Center Press, 1989

Richard Strozzi

The Anatomy of Change: East/West Approaches to Body/Mind Therapy: Shambhala, 1984
Holding the Center: Sanctuary in a Time of Confusion: Frog Books, 1997

Further Resources – Beyond The Books:

Workshops and Personal Programs

Dr. Joseph Riggio

- **Foolish Wisdom** - Focused transformational with Joseph workshops for personal change and evolution, delivered live and via simulcast
- **Leadership Wisdom & L3|Leadership Learning Laboratory** - Professional development for executives, entrepreneurs, business owners and professionals
- **Unconventional Advice Private Access** – Private consulting, coaching, mentoring and membership programs for personal development and professional advice
- **NLP Consulting Certification Training** – with Dr. Joseph Riggio currently available from ABTI | Princeton in association with the Society of NLP | Richard Bandler
- **MythoSelf Professional Training** – certification training directly with Dr. Joseph Riggio in the most intense, experiential, transformational process currently available from ABTI | Princeton

Get more information about these programs at:
http://www.JosephRiggio.com/programs

Audio & Video Resources

NOTE: The following are some of products available at:

http://www.josephriggio.com/products

- and -

http://www.tools4consciousevolution.com

Dr. Joseph Riggio

- *TCP | The Complete Package*
- *Precision Hypnosis*

- *Million-Dollar Business Building*
- *EPC Series One: Exquisite Performance Consulting*
- *Beyond the Obvious: Introduction to Exquisite Performance Consulting*
- *BEYOND ... Series: Beyond NLP, Beyond Hypnosis, Beyond NLP 2, Beyond Belief*
- *Seven Secrets of Wealth Attraction Success*
- *Story Control w/Jamie Smart - Audio*
- *POWER! - Audio, Video and Transcripts*
- *The MythoSelf Process: Taipei 2010 - Audio & Transcripts*
- *The MythoSelf Archives 1999-2010 - Digital eBook Compilation*
- *INFLUENCE!*
- *Adv. Patterns of Persuasion and Influence: Hypnosis Master Class*
- *Advanced Somatics*
- *Advanced Semantics*
- *The Book of Ancient Secrets*

Dr. Richard Bandler

- *NeuroSonics: Personal Enhancement Series*
- *Ferocious Resolve*
- *Wanton Motivation*
- *Hurdling Hesitation*
- *Unfearing Decisions and Soften More*
- *Persuasion Engineering w/John LaValle*
- *DHE: Design Human Engineering w/John LaValle*

Brain Technologies On-Line Assessments
NOTE: Follow up consultation with Dr. Joseph Riggio is also available

- *BrainMap - Dudley Lynch*

- *Yo!Dolphin! – Dudley Lynch & Paul Kordis*
- *Asset Report – Dudley Lynch*

Websites

http://www.JosephRiggio.com
Dr. Joseph Riggio's personal website where you'll find many free articles, audios and videos on his blog, Blognostra; as well as complete information about his programs and products ... and much more.

http://www.JosephRiggio.tv
This is Dr. Joseph Riggio's personal multi-media site with free video resources, a live interactive video chat room and private coaching and training access, including Joseph's unique live Internet simulcast programs.

http://www.GenerativeNLP.com
A site with a wealth of information about all things MythoSelf including many MythoSelf based articles and products, run by Licensed MythoSelf Trainer, Charles Moore.

http://www.HeroPathForTeens.com
Master MythoSelf Trainer Jeffrey Leiken, M.A. manages this site with articles relevant to and about the HeroPath program for teens based on the MythoSelf Process.

http://www.AcuityWorld.com
Acuity World is the home of Henrik Wenoe a leading NLP institute providing high-level training and consulting in Denmark, including Master Classes and intensive Summer Training programs with Dr. Joseph Riggio.

http://www.PureNLP.com
This is the primary site of NLP Seminars International run by John La Valle. You'll find information about Society of NLP training, and links to dozens of NLP resources.

http://www.RichardBandler.com
Richard Bandler's primary website ... latest news, videos and Richard's training schedule.

About The Author

Joseph Riggio, Ph.D.

Joseph Riggio, architect and designer of the **MythoSelf® Process** and **Soma-Semantics®** is a leading figure in international personal and professional development circles. As a Master NLP Trainer and Hypnotist he is acclaimed for the breadth, depth and precision of his expertise as a transformational change artist. Among the consultants, coaches and clients Joseph has trained and worked with his skill in the utilization of somatics is renowned, as are his use of hypnotic language, metaphor and storytelling.

> "A very powerful piece for me is how Joe leads with the body in the changework he does. He actually worked with me muscle-by-muscle to reach my desired physical state, connecting it firmly to the mental changes when they began. though others have used kinesthesia as an entree into changework, Joe was more thorough and complete than anyone else I've worked with. He really understands musculature and physiology, and uses his knowledge expertly.
>
> Balance was my theme. Physically, we actually changed the way I walked. I now have a calmer, more assured, balanced way of walking. Mentally, I developed the ability to orient myself to the world differently. I have increasing access to a way of being that lets me

peacefully take in more information with less effort and internal chatter. I'm handling life by letting me let go of the irrelevancies and attend only to what's important in reaching my goals. The state isn't perfect, yet; I must often remember to get. back there. But the workshop created and gave me access to a new level of resources."

- Stever Robbins, M.B.A. Harvard, Society of NLP™ Elite Master Trainer

While Dr. Riggio is well know and well regarded for his work developing new transformational performance methods and technology, he is probably most widely known as a keynote speaker and workshop leader. Joseph has run programs around the world for clients seeking profound personal, professional and organizational transformation and performance improvement.

A highly regarded professional consultant, coach and mentor, Joseph has worked with leading Fortune 100 International companies and thousands of executives within them. Dr. Riggio's proprietary training programs in sales and leadership development have been delivered in over thirty countries and translated into more than ten languages.

"I contracted with Joseph in 2000 for a long term process; at first instance we collaborated over a 3 years period with multiple trainings of our global sales & marketing organization. This process was pivotal in bringing our organization to the expected level and supported other initiatives resulting in extraordinary sales results and increased customer satisfaction. Joseph is a brilliant trainer, coach and process facilitator going far to share his talent and competencies simultaneously with acting in multicultural environment and providing training for us in 7 different langue's (Danish, German, English, French, Italian, Japanese, and Spanish). A true master with high integrity"

Else Beth Trautner, CEO at Euro-Diagnostica AB

Dr. Riggio has developed seminal work in the area of applied mythology related to personal and professional development, especially as it applies to decision-making, performance and leadership. The fundamental technology that Joseph continues to develop is sensorially and aesthetically organized transcending the limitations of ordinary cortical cognition. His interest if focused on understanding and utilizing the sub-cortical processes of implicit learning in what he refers to as the "*Silent Brain.*"

More than twenty years of developing the essential material that comprises the **MythoSelf Process** work and **Soma-Semantics** model led Joseph to producing **TCP | The Complete Package**, a multi-media program clients can use on their own, designed to create the kind of transformational results he is renowned for generating with clients in his workshops and when doing private work with them.

"*I just got TCP | The Complete Package yesterday and have listened to it couple times now. I really enjoyed it. The whole design is easy to use, the background music is upbeat and cheerful and most importantly, the content of the audio and video are amazing. I was having some trouble with a client and wasn't sure how I was going to interact with her on our next meeting and I followed the audio and it just led me and reset my ways of being effortlessly and I met the client and the meeting went exactly the way I wanted it. As it said in TCP | The Complete Package, like this, EVERYTHING IS POSSIBLE. I am very pleased about what this product did for me and I look forward to what it can do for me now and in the future. I recommend TCP | The Complete Package to those who want to produce significant and tangible results in life!*"

– Vivian Wang, HongLi International Consulting Studio, Taipei, Taiwa

Also from Joseph Riggio:

**The State of Perfection
Your Hidden Code to Unleashing Personal Mastery**

BOOK DESCRIPTION (from the Back Cover):

For the first time in print Dr. Riggio divulges the true power of the MythoSelf Process, including how to access and operate from the "Ready State" – a highly charged positive bias that is the difference between mediocre and elite performers. Utilizing clear and precise explanation, Dr. Riggio walks you through the methodology and technology behind the MythoSelf Process, allowing you reconnect with your state of perfection.

Through this process you will access and express yourself naturally and effortlessly. The State of Perfection will provide you with a newfound, unshakable confidence in yourself and your ability to create extraordinary results in your life, as well as how to remain in charge, calm, cool and collected, especially in times of crisis and in the face of chaos.

PRAISE FOR The State of Perfection: Your Hidden Code to Unleashing Personal Mastery

"An Incredible Journey."

"After 20-years, Joseph Riggio has finally found the formula to convey in a book what he does in his personal work."

"Most personal improvement books begin with the assumption that the reader is somehow damaged and needs to be "fixed." Joseph Riggio starts out with the belief in great potential and sends the reader on an incredible journey." - Alan Weiss, PhD Best-selling author, Million Dollar Consulting & Million Dollar Coaching

"A unique and powerful process for transformational change." - John La Valle Co-author of Persuasion Engineering®, President of the Society of NLP™ "Beware! This book will change your life".

"In The State of Perfection Joseph Riggio operates on so many cleverly interwoven levels that it cannot fail to transform whoever reads it. From the moment you turn the first page you will find yourself willingly going down the rabbit hole of your deepest desires, entranced by Dr. Riggio's exquisitely woven tapestry of masterful and entertaining metaphorical stories, superb hypnotic and linguistic skills combined with the powerful experience of being in the seminar room with one of the greatest personal transformation facilitators of all time."

"*A masterpiece of its kind, The State of Perfection is set to become the #1 self-help book of all time. Ignore it at your peril!*" - Peta Heskell, Best Selling UK Author and Society of NLP™ Licensed Trainer

"*Rarely is the curtain of life thrust aside to reveal the elusive truths*" "*What is the meaning of life? The clues are within the secret paths of consciousness – our personal program for excellence - but few can read the* map... until now. Rarely is the curtain of life thrust aside to reveal the elusive truths of self... Dr. Joseph Riggio's new book, 'The State of Perfection: Your Hidden Code to Unleashing Personal Mastery' is the guide and you are the treasure!" - W.L. Hoffman, J.D. – Author of "The Soulstealer War"

"Refreshingly Innovative."

"Unlike the countless volumes written on self-understanding and mastery, which often focus on understanding past traumas and their impact on the dilemmas you are currently facing, Joseph begins from an entirely different, refreshingly innovative premise: you already work perfectly; you've just forgotten what that's like and how to retrieve the state in which it occurs. Drawing upon the ideas of some notable and influential people in his life—Joseph Campbell, Richard Bandler and most eminently, Roye Fraser, Dr. Riggio synthesized some of their ideas with his own to create the Mythoself Process." - Randy W. Green, PhD

The State of Perfection: Your Hidden

Code to Unleashing Personal Mastery

available at: **Amazon.com**

and other fine book retailers.

www.ingramcontent.com/pod-product-compliance
Lightning Source LLC
Chambersburg PA
CBHW022110150426
43195CB00008B/345